SELECTED WORKS OF

RUMI

FP

CLASSICS

Published 2025

FiNGERPRINT! **CLASSiCS**

Prakash Books

📘 Fingerprint Publishing
𝕏 @FingerprintP
📷 @fingerprintpublishingbooks
www.fingerprintpublishing.com

ISBN: 978 93 6214 383 9

Not from books, not from speech,
But from love, the soul will reach.

Lose yourself, let ego burn,
To the fire, you will return.

He spoke of longing, pain, and flight,
Of hearts that break to hold the light.

Come, be silent, feel the glow,
What you seek, you already know.

J alal al-Din Rumi's poetry has transcended centuries, cultures, and languages, finding a home in the hearts of people worldwide. His words, filled with longing, wisdom, and devotion, speak to something universal in the human experience. Whether in moments of joy or sorrow, love or loss, readers turn to his verses for comfort, inspiration, and self-discovery.

But what makes Rumi's poetry classic yet contemporary? His work is not merely literature but rather an invitation to explore the mysteries of the soul. He urges readers to move beyond rigid beliefs, embrace uncertainty, and surrender to love's transformative power. His verses because they remind us that true fulfillment is not found in external achievements but in an awakened heart.

Born in 1207 in present-day Afghanistan, Rumi was raised in a family of scholars. His father, Baha al-Din Walad, was a respected theologian, and Rumi was expected to follow in his footsteps. Immersed in Islamic law, philosophy, and religious scholarship from an early age, he gained widespread admiration as a teacher.

For years, he lived as a conventional scholar in Konya, then a major intellectual center of the Seljuq Empire. His reputation grew, and he attracted students drawn to his eloquence and knowledge. Yet beneath this scholarly exterior, a deeper spiritual yearning was taking root.

That yearning found its catalyst in 1244 when he met Shams of Tabriz, a wandering mystic who would change his life forever. Their connection was immediate and a deep one. Shams, uninterested in academic knowledge, sought a direct, personal experience of the divine. He challenged Rumi to move beyond intellect and embrace a more ecstatic, unfiltered spirituality.

This encounter sparked a radical transformation. Rumi, once a revered theologian, turned to mystical poetry, dance, and music as expressions of devotion. His writing became infused with passion, reflecting the intensity of his newfound spiritual journey.

At the core of Rumi's poetry is longing—not just romantic but existential. He saw love as a force that shapes existence, a path to transcendence:

> "I was dead, then alive.
> Weeping, then laughing.
> The power of love came into me,
> And I became fierce like a lion,
> Then tender like the evening star."

For Rumi, love was an all-consuming fire that burned away the ego, leaving behind only the purity of the heart. Even the mysterious disappearance of Shams—believed by some to be an assassination—only deepened Rumi's poetic expression. His grief found voice in *Diwan-e Shams-e Tabrizi,* where personal sorrow transformed into universal longing.

While deeply rooted in Sufi thought, Rumi's poetry transcends religious divisions. His vision of spirituality is inclusive, recognizing the divine in all places and people. He challenges narrow interpretations of faith, urging readers to experience the divine through love, surrender, and inner awakening. This openness is why his words resonate across cultures, offering wisdom to anyone searching for meaning and belonging.

Rumi's poetry is not just memorable for its themes but for how he expresses them. His verses, rich with metaphors, paradoxes, and playful imagery, make truths feel both accessible and engaging. He does not preach but invites. He does not dictate but awakens. His language remains vivid yet unpretentious, philosophical yet deeply personal. Whether speaking of a wandering dervish, a drunken tavern-goer, or a yearning lover, his poetry captures the full range of human emotion, making the reader feel part of the journey.

Moreover, his storytelling, often humorous and unexpected, serves a deeper purpose. As scholar Leonard Lewisohn noted, Rumi frequently employs unconventional narratives to prompt readers to question their assumptions about spirituality, ethics, and life itself. In an age marked by division and uncertainty, his words offer an alternative vision:

> "Out beyond ideas of wrongdoing and rightdoing,
> there is a field. I'll meet you there."

Even for those who do not follow a spiritual path, Rumi's words resonate because they address fundamental human concerns: the search for meaning, the desire to love and be loved, and the courage to embrace the unknown.

Rumi's voice continues to echo across time, his verses recited at weddings, inscribed on walls, and shared in moments of both heartbreak and joy. His poetry is not about certainty but about wonder, not about possession but surrender. His words whisper to the soul, urging us to let go of fear and embrace the fullness of existence. They remind us that the journey is not about reaching a destination but about embracing the mystery of love and the beauty of being.

Centuries may pass, but as long as human hearts continue to seek, Rumi's words will guide them home.

References:

1. Qamber, Akhtar. "Rumi: Mystic Extraordinary." India International Centre Quarterly 15, no. 3 (1988): 103–16.
2. Mannani, Manijeh. "THE METAPHYSICS OF THE HEART IN THE SUFI POETRY OF RUMI." Religion & Literature 42, no. 3 (2010): 161–68.

CONTENTS

THE ORIGIN
OF SUFISM

Among the Mohammedans Súfíism, or Persian mysticism, is known as tasawwuf. The word Sidi is derived from súf, meaning "wool." When a little Persian sect at the end of the eighth century A.D. broke away from the orthodox Muslim religion, and struck out on an independent path, they ignored costly robes and worldly ostentation, and clad themselves in a white wool garment. Hence they were known as "wool wearers," or Súfís.

Prof. Edward G. Browne gives four theories in regard to the origin of Súfíism, viz.: (1) Esoteric Doctrine of the Prophet.(2) Reaction of the Aryan mind against a Semitic religion. (3) Neo-Platonist influence.(4) Independent origin. Neither of the four theories altogether satisfies the learned professor, and very certain it is that the last-mentioned theory is of very little account. Prof. Browne seems in favour of a "spontaneous growth" existing in various forms, under various names throughout the civilised world; but after all this is not very tangible evidence. Moreover, we must bear in mind that the Neo-Platonist philosophers paid a visit to the Persian court in the sixth century A.D., and founded a school there in the reign of Núshír-wan. It is highly probable, therefore, that these seven philosophers, forced to leave their homes through the tyranny of Justinian, who forbade the teaching of philosophy at Athens, should have had considerable influence upon a few of the more thoughtful Persians. We shall now find that this theory is borne out by internal evidence.

Let us briefly study the tenets of Neo-Platonism. The Neo-Platonists believed in the Supreme Good as the Source of all things. Self-existent, it generated from itself. Creation was the reflection of its own Being. Nature, therefore, was permeated with God. Matter was essentially non-existent, a temporary and ever-moving shadow for the embodiment of the Divine. The Neo-Platonists believed that by ecstasy and contemplation of the All-Good, man would rise to that Source from whence he came. These points bear directly upon the Súfí teaching. They form a broad outline of the tenets of Súfíism. The Súfís, from temperamental and other causes, elaborated these ideas, gave them a rich and beautiful setting, and, what is all-important, built about them one of the most interesting phases of mystical poetry the world has ever known, and this particular phase may be said to date from the twelfth century A.D.

Thus, I think, it will be readily admitted that the Súfís certainly owed something to the Neo-Platonists. The cry for the Beloved was in their hearts before the Greek philosophers came; but Neo-Platonism appealed to their Oriental minds. It was a stepping-stone across the river of their particular spiritual tendencies, and they trod thereon, and proceeded to lay down other stones across the stream. I have pointed out the similarities between this particular Greek and Persian belief. There was, however, one very important difference. The Neo-Platonist's conception of God was purely abstract, the Súfí's essentially personal, as far as the early Súfís were concerned. We shall consider other influences which were brought to bear upon Súfíism a little later on. There is a very great difference between the early Súfíism and the elaborate additions that followed as an evolutionary matter of course.

In brief, then, Neo-Platonism was the doctrine of Ecstasy. A quotation from the letter of Plotinus to Flaccus on Ecstasy will still further show the similarities between this Greek and Persian teaching:

"The wise man recognises the idea of the Good within him. This he develops by withdrawal into the Holy Place of his own soul. He who does not understand how the soul contains the Beautiful within itself, seeks to realise beauty without, by laborious production. His aim should rather be to concentrate and simplify, and so to expand his being; instead of going out into the Manifold, to forsake it for the One, and so to float upwards towards the Divine Fount of Being whose stream flows within him."

This is Súfiism in prose. The Súfí turned the same conception into poetry.

A NOTE ON
PERSIAN POETRY

NĪZAMĪ'S DISCOURSE
ON POETRY

In Nīzamī's The Chahár Magála ("Four Discourses"), translated by Professor Edward G. Browne, we find the Second Discourse devoted to "The Nature of Poetry, and the Utility of the Skilful Poet." In this interesting Discourse Nīzamī very amiably discusses the training required to become a poet of enduring fame, and intersperses these remarks with a number of anecdotes, which in the main are examples of the advantages derived from poetic improvisations given at opportune moments before kings when wine has gone round two or three times. Nīzamī sums up the nature of poetry in the following words: "Poetry is that art whereby the poet arranges imaginary propositions and adapts the deductions, with the result that he can make a little thing appear great and a great thing small, or cause good to appear in the garb of evil and evil in the garb of good." Nīzamī denounces the habit of giving money to old poets. He remarks: "For one so ignoble as not to have discovered in fifty years that what he writes is bad, when will he discover it?" On the other hand Nīzamī favours the young poet with hopeful talent, and generously remarks that "it is proper to patronise him, a duty to take care of him, and an obligation to maintain him." The minor poets of to-day have not these glowing advantages!

The most ingenious example of a poetic improvisation in this Discourse is, perhaps, one given by Rúdagí in connection with the protracted stay of Amír Nasr b. Ahmad in Herát. Four years the Amír camped with his army in this town, with its twenty different varieties of grape and beautiful narcissus. "He preferred Herát to the Garden of Eden." But at length the Amír's captains and courtiers grew weary of being absent so long from Bukhárá, where they longed to see their wives and children again. They offered Rúdagí, the poet, five thousand dinars if he could persuade the Amír to quit Herát and return to Bukhárá. Rúdagí, at an opportune moment, took up his harp and sang the following song to the Amír:

> *The sands of Oxus, toilsome though they be,*
> *Beneath my feet were soft as silk to me.*
> *Glad at the friend's return, the Oxus deep*
> *Up to our girths in laughing waves shall leap.*
> *Long live Bukhárá! Be thou of good cheer!*
> *Joyous towards thee hasteth our Amír!*
> *The Moon's the Prince, Bukhárá, is the sky;*
> *O sky, the Moon shall light thee by and bye!*
> *Bukhárá, is the mead, the Cypress he;*
> *Receive at last, O Mead, thy Cypress-tree!*

This particular Amír seems to have been fond of flattery, and he found the daintily turned song of Rúdagí more acceptable to his vanity than even the beauty of Herát. He accordingly took his departure immediately the song had concluded, and, in his absent-mindedness, forgot to put on his boots, which were carried by an attendant who rode in hot pursuit.

Poetry in those days was evidently a remunerative pursuit. Nīzamī tells us that Khidr Khán always had in readiness four trays of gold. "These he used to dispense by the handful" to the successful poets. Though the royal favour towards the poets was extremely bountiful, Persian poets were not always particularly courteous the one to the other. Nīzamī tells an amusing story of a minor poet named Rashídí. At the king's command the Poet-Laureate was asked to express his opinion of Rashídí's poetry. The Poet-Laureate accordingly remarked: "His verse is extremely good and chaste and correct, but it wants spice." The king afterwards repeated these words to Rashídí and bade him compose a fitting rejoinder. Rashídí composed the following verse:

You stigmatise my verse as "wanting spice,"
And possibly, my friend, you may be right.
My verse is honey-flavoured, sugar-sweet,
And spice with such could scarcely cause delight.
Spice is for you, you blackguard, not for me,
For beans and turnips is the stuff you write!

This was not kind; but Rashídí received all four baskets of gold that day!

The technical study of prosody was instituted by Khalil ibn i Ahmad i Bicrí. He is said to have discovered this science by listening to the rythmic beats of the fuller's mallets upon his clothes. This story is mentioned in Saifi's Treatise on Prosody.

Much of Persian poetry is conventional, and the demarcation in style, due to the various phases of Persian history, is not as pronounced as might be expected. The Persian poets not only conservatively followed old metres, but old similes, old subjects as well. It was with words they were most concerned, and not with ideas. The Lover's Companion of Sharafu'd-Dín Rámí is sufficient to prove this. The book contains a very large number of similes on the various parts of the body. This was intended to be a vade mecum to the writer of erotic poetry. Professor Brown defends this conservatism and remarks that it has "guarded the Persian language from the vulgarisation which the triumph of an untrained, untrammelled, and unconventional genius of the barbaric-degenerate type tends to produce in our own and other European tongues."

THE LIFE
AND WORK OF
JALÁLU'D-DÍN RÚMÍ

I

LIFE

Jalálu'd-Dín Rúmí was born at Balkh on September 30th, 1207, A.D., or according to Mohammedan reckoning, in 604 A.H. His father, Bahaū-'d-Dín, was a man of much learning, but gave offence to the reigning king by an attack on that monarch's innovations. Another account disputes this in the place of jealousy on the part of the king. Whatever the cause, however, Bahaū-'d-Dín left Balkh, together with his family, and settled at Nishapur. It was here that the celebrated Súfí, Farídu'd-Dín 'Attár, presented young Jalálu'd-Dín Rúmí with his Asrarnama, and informed his father that the child would some day become famous throughout the world. After the destruction of Balkh the family went to Qonia, an old Roman province, where the poet acquired his name Rúmí, or "the Roman." Young Jalál must have been a child prodigy if we are to believe the many wonderful stories of his early days. At six years of age he is said to have seen visions, taught his playmates philosophy, and performed many marvellous feats, such as flying into the celestial regions. On the death of his father Jalál took the professorial chair. He also founded an order of Dervishes known as Maulavis, where he authorised music and religious dance. When asked why he introduced singing and dance at a funeral, such practice being contrary to custom, Jalál replied: "When the human spirit, after years of imprisonment in the cage and dungeon of the body, is at length set free, and wings its flight to the Source whence it came, is not this an occasion for rejoicings, thanks, and dancing?" Jalál was an indomitable optimist. In his sayings, and still more in his poetry, we find an almost untrammelled ecstasy. The religious dances, known as Rizā Kulī, may in some way account for Jalál's occasional lack of care displayed in his poetry, and also for the outbursts not far removed from insanity. We are informed by Daulat Sháh that "There was a pillar in the Maulavi's house, and when he was drowned in the ocean of Love he used to take hold of that pillar and set himself turning round it." It was while turning round the pillar that he not infrequently dictated much of his poetry. As Mr. Arthur Symons has sung:

> *I turn until my sense,*
> *Dizzied with waves of air,*
> *Spins to a point intense,*
> *And spires and centres there.*

We can well imagine Jalál writing the following under the conditions just mentioned:

> *"Come! Come! Thou art the Soul, the Soul so dear, revolving!*
> *Come! Come! Thou art the Cedar, the Cedar's Spear, revolving!*
> *Oh, come! The well of Light up-bubbling springs;*
> *And Morning Stars exult, in Gladness sheer, revolving!"*

In 1226 A.D. Jalál was married at Lerenda to Gevher (Pearl). She bore two sons and died early in life. Jalál married again and his second wife survived him.

II

SHAMSI TABRIZ

A word must now be said about Shamsi Tabríz, an intimate friend of Jalál. We have sufficient evidence to prove that Shamsi Tabríz, Jalál's nom de guerre, was an actual person, and not a mythical creation on the part of the poet. This mysterious being, who flitted across Jalál's life so tragically, seems to have had great personal influence over the poet, who went with him into solitary places and there discussed profound mysteries. The scholars of Jalál looked upon the whole affair as an unworthy infatuation on the part of their Master, and on the part of Shams a shameful seduction. Their protests brought about the flight of Shams, who fled to Tabríz. But it was only a momentary separation. Jalál followed this strange figure and brought him back again. Most of his lighter poetry was composed during this separation. Another disturbance, however, caused the departure of Shams to Damascus. We then have no clear record of him. Various legends exist in regard to the death of this mysterious person. It may be safely stated, however, that Shams met with a violent death, the exact nature of which it is impossible to say definitely.

This strange union is by no means unique in the history of the world's literature. The union, however, in this particular case, is extremely difficult to rightly fathom. We may reasonably infer that Jalál's intense poetic temperament became fascinated by the dogmatic and powerful Shams. The very treatment of this friendship, both in the Lyrical Poems, and in the Masnavi, is Súfí The two following quotations, from many that might be cited, will prove sufficient to illustrate this point:

The face of Shamsi Dín, Tabríz's glory, is the sun
In whose track the cloud-like hearts are moving.

O Shamsi Tabríz, beauty and glory of the horizons,
What king but is a beggar of thee with heart and soul?

III

THE STORIES OF AL-AFLĀKÍ AND THE
DEATH OF JALÁLU'D-DÍN RÚMÍ.

The historian al-Aflākí, in his collection of anecdotes called Menaqibu 'L 'Arifin, gives a number of stories relating to the miracles and wise sayings of Jalál. Many of these miraculous performances were followed by the conversion of those who witnessed them. A marvel or a wise saying of Jalál was generally accompanied by music and dance, which reminds us of the jubilations of the Indian gods after Rama's victories over his enemies. These stories, interesting enough in themselves, can scarcely be credited to such a learned man as Jalál undoubtedly was. According to tradition he spoke to frogs and fishes, raised the dead to life, and at the same time very ignominiously lost his temper when a disciple who said, after having received Jalál's instructions: "God willing." After all, the significance of Jalál lies not in these rather lamentable fairy tales, but in the fruit of his work. Jalál, like the Lord Buddha, suffered considerably from the addition of fabulous tales and fancies of no real moment to his teachings.

Al-Aflākí tells a pretty story concerning the tenderness of Jalál for little children. As the poet passed by some children, they left their play and ran to him and bowed. Jalál bowed in response. One little boy, some distance off, seeing the honour bestowed upon his playmates, cried to Jalál: "Wait for me until I come!" And Jalál waited and bowed to the little child. This story is worth far more than juggler's tricks.

Jalálu'd-Dín Rúmí died at Qonia in 1273 A.D., praising God and leaving to the world a vast store of spiritual knowledge and many wise instructions to his son, Bahaū-'d-Dín Valad. It is very gratifying to note that at the death of Jalál his mourners were of all creeds. A Christian was asked why he wept over a Muslim grave, and he replied: "We esteem him as the Moses, the David, the Jesus of our time; and we are his disciples, his adherents." This was indeed a splendid and worthy tribute to the memory of so great a man.

I hope I have already demonstrated that the very nature of Súfí poetry is entirely lacking in creed or dogma, and certainly the great singer of the Masnavi has left in his songs a wealth of the wonder of Divine Love.

IV

THE NATURE AND SIGNIFICANCE OF JALÁLU'D-DÍN RÚMÍ'S POETRY

The Lyrical.—We have already noted the acceptance of the Asrarnama. Among the other literary influences, according to Mr. Nicholson, we may note the poems of Sana'í, Sa'di, and Nīzamī. The fact that Jalál's poetry sometimes faintly resembles Omar Khayyám's is too slight to be of any value. Mr. Nicholson very ably sums up the nature of the Masnavi and Divan respectively: "The one is a majestic river, calm and deep, meandering through many a rich and varied landscape to the immeasurable ocean; the other a foaming

torrent that leaps and plunges in the ethereal solitude of the hills."
The poetry of Jalál is not of equal merit. His work seldom if ever
has the technical polish of Jámí. There is too much of it; too much
produced in the belief that all his poetry was inspired. He is fond of
harping on certain words, and as far as the translations are concerned
he has little sense of humour. There was certainly room for a touch
of humour in the poet's description of Iblis receiving from God
a gift of beautiful women whereby to tempt mankind; but Jalál
entirely ignores it. These weaknesses are almost lost in the strength
and purity and lyrical grandeur of many of Jalál's poems. He carries
us along on a torrent of heavenly music. The rhythmic, swing of
his wonderful dance is soul-stirring. We seem to move exultantly,
ecstatically, to the sound of the poet's singing, far behind the silver
stars into the Presence of the Beloved. With what reverence, with
what a glow of simile and subtle suggestion he describes the Beauty
of the Beloved! With what exquisite passion he foretells the Eternal
Union! Then there is a lull in this fierce spiritual song, and Jalál
sings, ever so gently and with an infinite tenderness, about human
tears being turned into "rain-clouds." He sings about the meeting
of two friends in Paradise, with the oft-repeated refrain, "Thou and
I." There seems in this poem an indescribable and almost pathetic
play on the idea of human friendship and the Divine Friendship, a
yearning tenderness for that human shadow, passing shadow though
it be. Jalál appears to have the power of producing almost orchestral
effects in his music of the Spheres. There is that terrific touch of
Wagner about his poetry, and in those suggestive Wagner-pauses
there is a tenderness of expression more touching, more truly great
than the loud triumphant notes. Jalál has truly said: "Our journey is
to the Rose-Garden of Union." He sang about, the Divine Rose-
Garden; but he did not forget to sing about the roses that fade and
the human hearts that ache. We seem to see Jalál ever bowing to the
little child in all his wonderful singing.

The Masnavi.—Jalál is said to have been forty-three years engaged in writing the Masnavi. Often whole nights were spent in its composition, Jalál reciting and his friend Hasam copying it down and sometimes singing portions of the verse in his beautiful voice. At the completion of the first book Hasam's wife died, and two years elapsed before the work was continued. The Masnavi is full of profound mysteries, and is a most important book in the study of Súfíism— mysteries which must, for the most part, be left to the discernment of the reader. Jalál himself has said that great Love is silent. It is in Silence that we shall come to understand the supreme Mystery of Love that has no comparison. The key-note to the Masnavi may be found in the Prologue to the first book. The poet here sings of the soul's longing to be united with the Beloved. The fact that he, and all other Súfí poets, use as an analogy the love between man and woman renders the spiritual meaning extremely vague. We have, however, already considered this point in the introduction, and it needs no further explanation. The Masnavi has all the pantheistic beauty of the Psalms, the music of the hills, the colour and scent of roses, the swaying of forests; but it has considerably more than that. These things of scent and form and colour are the Mirror of the Beloved; these earthy loves the journey down the valley into the Rose-Garden where the roses never fade, and where Love is.

SELECTIONS FROM
THE MASNAVI

SORROW QUENCHED
IN THE BELOVED

Through grief my days are as labour and sorrow,
My days move on, hand in hand with anguish.
Yet, though my days vanish thus, 'tis no matter,
Do Thou abide, O Incomparable Pure One.

THE MUSIC OF LOVE

Hail to thee, then, O LOVE, sweet madness!
Thou who healest all our infirmities!
Who art the Physician of our pride and self conceit!
Who art our Plato and our Galen!
Love exalts our earthly bodies to heaven,
And makes the very hills to dance with joy!
O lover, 'twas Love that gave life to Mount Sinai,
When "it quaked, and Moses fell down in a swoon."
Did my Beloved only touch me with His lips,
I too, like a flute, would burst out into melody.

WHEN THE ROSE HAS FADED

When the rose has faded and the garden is withered,
The song of the nightingale is no longer to be heard.
The BELOVED is all in all, the lover only veils Him;
The BELOVED is all that lives, the lover a dead thing.
When the lover feels no longer LOVE'S quickening,
He becomes like a bird who has lost its wings. Alas!
How can I retain my senses about me,
When the BELOVED shows not the Light of His countenance?

THE SILENCE OF LOVE

Love is the astrolabe of God's mysteries.
A lover may hanker after this love or that love,
But at the last he is drawn to the KING of Love.
However much we describe and explain Love,
When we fall in love we are ashamed of our words.
Explanation by the tongue makes most things clear,
But Love unexplained is better.

EARTHLY LOVE ESSENTIAL
TO THE LOVE DIVINE

In one 'twas said, "Leave power and weakness alone;
Whatever withdraws thine eyes from God is an idol."

In one 'twas said, "Quench not thy earthy torch,
That it may be a light to lighten mankind.
If thou neglectest regard and care for it,
Thou wilt quench at midnight the lamp of Union."

THE ETERNAL SPLENDOUR
OF THE BELOVED

Why dost Thou flee from the cries of us on earth?
Why pourest Thou sorrow on the heart of the sorrowful?
O Thou who, as each new morn dawns from the east,
Art seen uprising anew, like a bright fountain!
What excuse makest Thou for Thy witcheries?
O Thou whose lips are sweeter than sugar,
Thou that ever renewest the life of this old world,
Hear the cry of this lifeless body and heart!

WOMAN

Woman is a ray of God, not a mere mistress,
The Creator's Self, as it were, not a mere creature!

THE DIVINE UNION

Mustafa became beside himself at that sweet call,
His prayer failed on "the night of the early morning halt."
He lifted not head from that blissful sleep,[1]

So that his morning prayer was put off till noon.
On that, his wedding night, in the presence of his bride,
His pure soul attained to kiss her hands.
Love and mistress are both veiled and hidden.
Impute it not a fault if I call Him "Bride."

HE KNOWS ABOUT IT ALL

He who is from head to foot a perfect rose or lily,
To him spring brings rejoicing.
The useless thorn desires the autumn,
That autumn may associate itself with the garden;
And hide the rose's beauty and the thorn's shame,
That men may not see the bloom of the one and the
other's shame;
That common stone and pure ruby may appear all as one.
True, the Gardener knows the difference in the autumn,
But the sight of One is better than the world's sight.

RESIGNATION THE WAY
TO PERFECTION

Whoso recognises and confesses his own defects
Is hastening in the way that leads to Perfection!
But he advances not towards the Almighty
Who fancies himself to be perfect.

LOVE THE SOURCE OF LIGHT
RATHER THAN VANISHING FORM

Whatsoever is perceived by sense He annuls,
But He stablishes that which is hidden from the senses.
The lover's love is visible, his Beloved hidden.
The Friend is absent, the distraction He causes present.
Renounce these affections for outward forms,
Love depends not on outward form or face.
Whatever is beloved is not a mere empty form,
Whether your beloved be of the earth or heaven.
Whatever is the form you have fallen in love with—
Why do you forsake it the moment life leaves it?
The form[2] is still there; whence then this disgust at it?
Ah! lover, consider well what is really your beloved.
If a thing perceived by outward senses is the beloved,
Then all who retain their senses must still love it;
And since Love increases constancy,
How can constancy fail while form abides?
But the truth is, the sun's beams strike the wall,
And the wall only reflects that borrowed light.
Why give your heart to mere stones, O simpleton?
Go! Seek the Source of Light which shineth alway!

THE RELIGION OF LOVE

The sect of lovers is distinct from all others,
Lovers have a religion and a faith of their own.

Though the ruby has no stamp, what matters it?
Love is fearless in the midst of the sea of fear.

PAIN IS A TREASURE!

Pain is a treasure, for it contains mercies;
The kernel is soft when the rind is scraped off.
O brother, the place of darkness and cold
Is the fountain of Life and the cup of ecstasy.
So also is endurance of pain and sickness and disease.
For from abasement proceeds exaltation.
The spring seasons are hidden in the autumns,
And the autumns are charged with springs.

SPIRIT GREATER THAN FORM

If spiritual manifestations had been sufficient,
The creation of the world had been needless and vain.
If spiritual thought were equivalent to love of God,
Outward forms of temples and prayers would not exist.

THE BELOVED COMPARED
TO A SWEET GARDEN

"We bow down our heads before His edict and ordinance,
We stake precious life to gain His favour.
While the thought of the Beloved fills our hearts,

All our work is to do Him service and spend life for Him.
Wherever He kindles His destructive torch,
Myriads of lovers' souls are burnt therewith.
The lovers who dwell within the sanctuary
Are moths burnt with the torch of the Beloved's face."
O heart, haste thither, for God will shine upon you,
And seem to you a sweet garden instead of a terror.
He will infuse into your soul a new Soul,
So as to fill you, like a goblet, with wine.
Take up your abode in His Soul!
Take up your abode in heaven, O bright full moon!
Like the heavenly Scribe, He will open your heart's book
That He may reveal mysteries unto you.

BEHOLD THE WATER
OF WATERS!

The sea itself is one thing, the foam another;
Neglect the foam, and regard the sea with your eyes.
Waves of foam rise from the sea night and day.
You look at the foam ripples and not at the mighty sea.
We, like boats, are tossed hither and thither,
We are blind though we are on the bright ocean.
Ah! you who are asleep in the boat of the body,
You see the water; behold the Water of waters!
Under the water you see there is another Water moving it.
Within the spirit is a Spirit that calls it.

* * * * *

When you have accepted the Light, O beloved,
When you behold what is veiled without a veil,
Like a star you will walk upon the heavens.

WHERE LOVE IS

A damsel said to her lover, "O fond youth,
You have visited many cities in your travels;
Which of those cities seems most delightful to you?"
He made answer, "The city wherein my love dwells,
In whatever nook my queen alights;
Though it be as the eye of a needle, 'tis a wide plain;
Wherever her Yusuf-like[3] face shines as a moon,
Though it be the bottom of a well, 'tis Paradise.
With thee, my love, hell itself were heaven.
With thee a prison would be a rose-garden.
With thee hell would be a mansion of delight,
Without thee lilies and roses would be as flames of fire!"

THE LOVE OF THE BELOVED

No lover ever seeks union with his beloved,
But his beloved is also seeking union with him.
But the lover's love[4] makes his body lean,
While the Beloved's love makes her fair and lusty.
When in this heart the lightning spark of love arises,
Be sure this Love is reciprocated in that heart.
When the Love of God arises in thy heart,
Without doubt God also feels love for thee.

THE LOVE OF THE SOUL AND THE LOVE
OF THE BODY

The Love of the soul is for Life and the Living One,
Because its origin is the Soul not bound to place.
The Love of the soul is for wisdom and knowledge,
That of the body for houses, gardens, and vine-yards;
The love of the soul is for things exalted on high,
That of the body for acquisition of goods and food.
The Love, too, of Him on high is directed to the soul:
Know this, for "He loves them that love Him."[5]
The sum is this: that whoso seeks another,
The soul of that other who is sought inclines to him.

O LOVE, LOVE, AND HEART'S
DESIRE OF LOVE!

Israfil of the resurrection-day of Love!
Love, Love, and heart's desire of Love!
Let thy first boon to me be this:
To lend thine ear to my orisons,
Though thou knowest my condition clearly,
O protector of slaves, listen to my speech.
A thousand times, O prince incomparable,
Has my reason taken flight in desire to see thee,
And to hear thee and to listen to thy words,
And to behold thy life-giving smiles.
Thy inclining thine ear to my supplications
Is as a caress to my misguided soul.

DESTROY NOT EARTHLY BEAUTY:
IT BEAUTIFIES THE SOUL

Tear not thy plumage off, it cannot be replaced;
Disfigure not thy face in wantonness, O fair one!
That face which is bright as the forenoon sun—
To disfigure it were a grievous sin.
'Twere paganism to mar such a face as thine
The moon itself would weep to lose sight of it!
Knowest thou not the beauty of thine own face?
Quit this temper that leads thee to war with thyself!
It is the claws of thine own foolish thoughts
That in spite wound the face of thy quiet soul.
Know such thoughts to be claws fraught with poison.
Which score deep wounds on the face of thy soul.

THE DEVIL MAKES USE
OF THE BEAUTY OF WOMEN

Thus spake cursed Iblis to the Almighty,
"I want a mighty trap to catch human game withal!"
God gave him gold and silver and troops and horses,
Saying, "You can catch my creatures with these."
Iblis said, "Bravo!" but at the same time hung his lip,
And frowned sourly like a bitter orange.
Then God offered gold and jewels from precious mines
To that laggard in the faith,
Saying, "Take these other traps, O cursed one."

But Iblis said, "Give me more, O blessed Defender."
God gave him succulent and sweet and costly wines,
And also store of silken garments.
But Iblis said, "O Lord, I want more aids than these,
In order to bind men in my twisted rope
So firmly that Thy adorers, who are valiant men,
May not, man-like, break my bonds asunder."

* * * * *

When at last God showed him the beauty of women,
Which bereaves men of reason and self-control,
Then Iblis clapped his hands and began to dance,
Saying, "Give me these; I shall quickly prevail with these!"[6]

LOVERS AND BELOVED HAVE BOTH PERISHED

Lovers and beloved have both perished;
And not themselves only, but their love as well.
'Tis God alone who agitates these nonentities,
Making one nonentity fall in love with another.
In the heart that is no heart envy comes to a head,
Thus Being troubles nonentity.[7]

O ANGELS, BRING HIM BACK TO ME

"O angels, bring him back to me.
Since the eyes of his heart were set on Hope,
Without care for consequence I set him free,
And draw the pen through the record of his sins!"

SELF-AGGRANDISEMENT AND VAINGLORY
NO PART OF LOVE

A lover was once admitted to the presence of his mistress, but, instead of embracing her, he pulled out a paper of sonnets and read them to her, describing her perfections and charms and his own love towards her at length. His mistress said to him, "You are now in my presence, and these lovers' sighs and invocations are a waste of time. It is not the part of a true lover to waste his time in this way. It shows that I am not the real object of your affection, but that what you really love is your own effusions and ecstatic raptures. I see, as it were, the water which I have longed for before me, and yet you withhold it. I am, as it were, in Bulgaria, and the object of your love is in Cathay. One who is really loved is the single object of her lover, the Alpha and Omega of his desires. As for you, you are wrapped up in your own amorous raptures, depending on the varying states of your own feelings, instead of being wrapped up in me."

I AM THINE, AND THOU ART MINE!

Eternal Life is gained by utter abandonment of one's own life. When God appears to His ardent lover the lover is absorbed in Him, and not so much as a hair of the lover remains. True lovers are as shadows, and when the sun shines in glory the shadows vanish away. He is a true lover to God to whom God says, "I am thine, and thou art Mine!"

LOVE NEEDS NO MEDIATOR

When one has attained Union with God he has no need of
intermediaries. Prophets and apostles are needed as links
to connect ordinary man with God, but he who hears the
"inner voice" within him has no need to listen to outward
words, even of apostles. Although that intercession is himself
dwelling in God, yet my state is higher and more lovely than
his. Though he is God's agent, yet I desire not his intercession
to save me from evil sent me by God, for evil at God's hand
seems to me good. What seems mercy and kindness to the
vulgar seems wrath and vengeance to God-intoxicated saints.

HUMANITY THE REFLECTION
OF THE BELOVED

Parrots are taught to speak without understanding the
words. The method is to place a mirror between the parrot
and the trainer. The trainer, hidden by the mirror, utters
the words, and the parrot, seeing his own reflection in the
mirror, fancies another parrot is speaking, and imitates all
that is said by the trainer behind the mirror. So God uses
prophets and saints as mirrors whereby to instruct men,
viz., the bodies of these saints and prophets; and men,
when they hear the words proceeding from these mirrors,
are utterly ignorant that they are really being spoken by
"Universal Reason" or the "Word of God" behind the
mirror of the saints.

EARTHLY FORMS

Earthly forms are only shadows of the Sun of Truth—a
cradle for babes, but too small to hold those who have
grown to spiritual manhood.

THE BEATIFIC VISION OF
ETERNAL TRUTH

The end and object of all negation is to attain to subsequent
affirmation, as the negation in the creed, "There is no
God," finds its complement and purpose in the affirmation
"but God." Just so the purpose of negation of self is to
clear the way for the apprehension of the fact that there is
no existence but the One. The intoxication of Life and its
pleasures and occupations veils the Truth from men's eyes,
and they ought to pass on to the spiritual intoxication which
makes men beside themselves and lifts them to the beatific
vision of eternal Truth.

THE WINE EVERLASTING

O babbler, while thy soul is drunk with mere date wine,
Thy spirit hath not tasted the genuine grapes.
For the token of thy having seen that divine Light
Is this, to withdraw thyself from the house of pride.

BE LOST IN THE BEAUTY
OF THE BELOVED

When those Egyptian women sacrificed their reason,
They penetrated the mansion of Joseph's love;
The Cup-bearer of Life bore away their reason,
They were filled with wisdom of the world without end.
Joseph's beauty was only an offshoot of God's beauty:
Be lost, then, in God's beauty more than those women.

WHAT EAR HAS TOLD YOU FALSELY

What ear has told you falsely eye will tell truly.
Then ear, too, will acquire the properties of an eye;
Your ears, now worthless as wool, will become gems;
Yea, your whole body will become a mirror,
It will be as an eye of a bright gem in your bosom.
First the hearing of the ear enables you to form ideas,
Then these ideas guide you to the Beloved.
Strive, then, to increase the number of these ideas,
That they may guide you, like Majnun, to the Beloved.

THERE IS A PLACE OF REFUGE

Yea, O sleeping heart, know the kingdom that endures not
For ever and ever is only a mere dream.

I marvel how long you will indulge in vain illusion,
Which has seized you by the throat like a heads man.
Know that even in this world there is a place of refuge;
Hearken not to the unbeliever who denies it.
His argument is this: he says again and again,
"If there were aught beyond this life we should see it."
But if the child see not the state of reason,
Does the man of reason therefore forsake reason?
And if the man of reason sees not the state of Love,
Is the blessed moon of Love thereby eclipsed?

THE LOVER'S
CRY TO THE BELOVED

"My back is broken by the conflict of my thoughts;
O Beloved One, come and stroke my head in mercy!
The palm of Thy hand on my head gives me rest,
Thy hand is a sign of Thy bounteous providence.
Remove not Thy shadow from my head,
I am afflicted, afflicted, afflicted!
Sleep has deserted my eyes
Through my longing for Thee, O Envy of cypresses!

* * * * *

O take my life, Thou art the Source of Life!
For apart from Thee I am wearied of my life.
I am a lover well versed in lovers' madness,
I am weary of learning and sense."

SORROW TURNED TO JOY

"He who extracts the rose from the thorn
Can also turn this winter into spring.
He who exalts the heads of the cypresses
Is able also out of sadness to bring joy."

THE GIFTS OF THE BELOVED

Where will you find one more liberal than God?
He buys the worthless rubbish which is your wealth,
He pays you the Light that illumines your heart.
He accepts these frozen and lifeless bodies of yours,
And gives you a Kingdom beyond what you dream of,
He takes a few drops of your tears,
And gives you the Divine Fount sweeter than sugar.
He takes your sighs fraught with grief and sadness,
And for each sigh gives rank in heaven as interest.
In return for the sigh-wind that raised tear-clouds,
God gave Abraham the title of "Father of the Faithful."

THOU ART HIDDEN FROM US

Thou art hidden from us, though the heavens are filled
With Thy Light, which is brighter than sun and moon!
Thou art hidden, yet revealest our hidden secrets
Thou art the Source that causes our rivers to flow.

Thou art hidden in Thy essence, but seen by Thy bounties.
Thou art like the water, and we like the mill-stone.
Thou art like the wind, and we like the dust;
The wind is unseen, but the dust is seen by all.
Thou art the Spring, and we the sweet green garden;
Spring is not seen, though its gifts are seen.
Thou art as the Soul, we as hand and foot;
Soul instructs hand and foot to hold and take.
Thou art as Reason, we like the tongue;
'Tis reason that teaches the tongue to speak.
Thou art as Joy, and we are laughing;
The laughter is the consequence of the joy.
Our every motion every moment testifies,
For it proves the presence of the Everlasting God.

EXERT YOURSELVES

"'Trust in God, yet tie the camel's leg.'
Hear the adage, 'The worker is the friend of God;'
Through trust in Providence neglect not to use means.
Go, O Fatalists, practise trust with self-exertion,
Exert yourself to attain your objects, bit by bit.
In order to succeed, strive and exert yourselves;
If you strive not for your objects, ye are fools."

THE WISDOM OF THE WEAK

"O friends, God has given me inspiration.
Oftentimes strong counsel is suggested to the weak.

The wit taught by God to the bee
Is withheld from the lion and the wild ass.
It fills its cells with liquid sweets,
For God opens the door of this knowledge to it.
The skill taught by God to the silkworm
Is a learning beyond the reach of the elephant.
The earthly Adam was taught of God names,
So that his glory reached the seventh heaven.
He laid low the name and fame of the angels,
Yet blind indeed are they whom God dooms to doubt!"

WHITE NIGHTS

Every night Thou freest our spirits from the body
And its snare, making them pure as rased tablets.
Every night spirits are released from this cage,
And set free, neither lording it nor lorded over.
At night prisoners are unaware of their prison,
At night kings are unaware of their majesty.

THE KINGLY SOUL

The kingly soul lays waste the body,
And after its destruction he builds it anew.
Happy the soul who for love of God
Has lavished family, wealth, and goods!—
Has destroyed its house to find the Hidden Treasure,
And with that Treasure has rebuilt it in fairer sort;

Has dammed up the stream and cleansed the channel,
And then turned a fresh stream into the channel.

SAINT AND HYPOCRITE

Watch the face of each one, regard it well,
It may be by serving thou wilt recognise Truth's face.
As there are many demons with men's faces,
It is wrong to join hand with every one.
When the fowler sounds his decoy whistle,
That the birds may be beguiled by that snare,
The birds hear that call simulating a bird's call,
And, descending from the air, find net and knife.
So vile hypocrites steal the language of Dervishes,
In order to beguile the simple with their trickery.
The works of the righteous are light and heat,
The works of the evil treachery and shamelessness.
They make stuffed lions to scare the simple,
They give the title of Muhammad to false Musailima.
But Musailima retained the name of "Liar,"
And Muhammad that of "Sublimest of beings."
That wine of God (the righteous) yields a perfume of musk;
Other wine (the evil) is reserved for penalties and pains.

HARSHNESS AND ADORATION

Let me then, I say, make complaint
Of the severity of that Fickle Fair One.
I cry, and my cries sound sweet in His ear;

He requires from the two worlds cries and groans.
How shall I not wail under His chastening hand?
How shall I not be in the number of those bewitched
by Him?
How shall I be other than night without His day?
Without the vision of His face that illumes the day?
His bitters are very sweets to my soul,
I am enamoured of my own grief and pain,
For it makes me well-pleasing to my peerless King
I use the dust of my grief as salve for my eyes,
That my eyes, like seas, may team with pearls.

THE DIVINE ABSORPTION

Do me justice, O Thou who art the glory of the just,
Who art the throne, and I the lintel of Thy door!
But, in sober truth, where are throne and door-way?
Where are "We" and "I"? There where our Beloved is!
O Thou, who art exempt from "Us" and "Me,"
Who pervadest the spirits of all men and women;
When man and woman become one, Thou art that One!
When their union is dissolved, lo! Thou abidest!
Thou hast made these "Us" and "Me" for this purpose,
To wit, to play chess with them by Thyself.
When Thou shalt become one entity with "Us" and "You,"
Then wilt Thou show true affection for these lovers.
When these "We" and "Ye" shall all become One Soul,
Then they will be lost and absorbed in the "Beloved."

LOVE MORE THAN SORROW
AND JOY

Come then, O Lord!
Who art exalted above description and explanation!
Is it possible for the bodily eye to behold Thee?
Can mind of man conceive Thy frowns and Thy smiles?
Are hearts, when bewitched by Thy smiles and frowns,
In a fit state to see the vision of Thyself?
When our hearts are bewitched by Thy smiles and frowns,
Can we gain Life from these two alternating states?
The fertile garden of Love, as it is boundless,
Contains other fruits besides joy and sorrow.
The true lover is exalted above these two states,
He is fresh and green independently of autumn or spring!
Pay tithe on Thy beauty, O Beauteous One!
Tell forth the tale of the Beloved, every whit!

THE HEART OF THE HARPER

The heart of the harper was emancipated.
Like a soul he was freed from weeping and rejoicing,
His old life died, and he was regenerated.
Amazement fell upon him at that moment,
For he was exalted above earth and heaven,
An uplifting of the heart surpassing all uplifting.
I cannot describe it; if you can, say on!
Ecstasy and words beyond all ecstatic words;—

Immersion in the glory of the Lord of glory!
Immersion wherefrom was no extrication,—
As it were identification with the Very Ocean!

WHEN NIGHT
RETURNS

When night returns and 'tis the time of the sky's levée,
The stars that were hidden come forth to their work.
The people of the world lie unconscious,
With veils drawn over their faces, and asleep;
But when the morn shall burst forth and the sun arise
Every creature will raise its head from its couch;
To the unconscious God will restore consciousness;
They will stand in rings as slaves with rings in ears;
Dancing and clapping hands with songs of praise,
Singing with joy, "Our Lord hath restored us to life!"

SEPARATION

Nothing is bitterer than severance from Thee,
Without Thy shelter there is naught but perplexity.
Our worldly goods rob us of our heavenly goods,
Our body rends the garment of our soul.
Our hands, as it were, prey on our feet;
Without reliance on Thee how can we live?

GOD'S LIGHT

'Tis God's Light that illumines the senses' light,
That is the meaning of "Light upon light."
The senses' light draws us earthwards.
God's Light calls us heavenwards.

LOVE CASTS ITS
OWN LIGHT

When love of God kindles a flame in the inward man,
He burns, and is freed from effects.
He has no need of signs to assure him of Love,
For Love casts its own Light up to heaven.

THE BELIEVER'S
HEART

The Prophet said that God has declared,
"I am not contained in aught above or below,
I am not contained in earth or sky, or even
In highest heaven. Know this for a surety, O beloved!
Yet am I contained in the believer's heart!
If ye seek Me, search in such hearts!"

SELF-SATISFACTION

No sickness worse than fancying thyself perfect
Can infect thy soul, O arrogant misguided one!
Shed many tears of blood from eyes and heart,
That this self-satisfaction may be driven out.
The fate of Iblis lay in saying, "I am better than He,"
And this same weakness lurks in the souls of all creatures.

TRUE KNOWLEDGE

The knowledge which is not of Him is a burden;
Knowledge which comes not immediately from Him
Endures no longer than the rouge of the tire-woman.
Nevertheless, if you bear this burden in a right spirit
'Twill be removed, and you will obtain joy.
See you bear not that burden out of vainglory,
Then you will behold a store of True Knowledge within.
When you mount the steed of this True Knowledge,
Straightway the burden will fall from your back.

THE FLAME OF LOVE

How long wilt thou dwell on words and superficialities?
A burning heart is what I want; consort with burning!
Kindle in thy heart the flame of Love,
And burn up utterly thoughts and fine expressions.

O Moses! the lovers of fair rites are one class,
They whose hearts and souls burn with Love another.

A MOTHER WHOSE CHILDREN WERE IN THE BELOVED'S KEEPING

A woman bore many children in succession, but none of them lived beyond the age of three or four months. In great distress she cried to God, and then beheld in a vision the beautiful gardens of Paradise, and many fair mansions therein, and upon one of these mansions she read her own name inscribed. And a voice from heaven informed her that God would accept the sorrows she had endured in lieu of her blood shed in holy war, as, owing to her sex, she was unable to go out to battle like the men. On looking again, the woman beheld in Paradise all the children she had lost, and she cried, "O Lord! they were lost to me, but safe with Thee!"

THE OPTIMISTIC ROSE

In this tale there is a warning for thee, O Soul,
That thou mayest acquiesce in God's ordinances,
And be wary and not doubt God's benevolence,
When sudden misfortune befalls thee.
Let others grow pale from fear of ill fortune,
Do thou smile like the rose at loss and gain;
For the rose, though its petals be torn asunder,
Still smiles on, and it is never cast down.

THE TRUE MOSQUE

Fools laud and magnify the mosque,
While they strive to oppress holy men of heart.
But the former is mere form, the latter spirit and truth.
The only true mosque is that in the hearts of saints.
The mosque that is built in the hearts of the saints
Is the place of worship of all, for God dwells there.
So long as the hearts of the saints are not afflicted.
God never destroys the nation.

IGNORANCE

Blood is impure, yet its stain is removed by water;
But that impurity of ignorance is more lasting,
Seeing that without the blessed water of God
It is not banished from the man who is subject to it.
O that thou wouldst turn thy face to thy own prayers,
And say, "Ah! my prayers are as defective as my being;
O requite me good for evil!"

A PRAYER

"Pray in this wise and allay your difficulties:
'Give us good in the house of our present world,
And give us good in the house of our next world.

Make our path pleasant as a garden,
And be Thou, O Holy One, our goal!'"

ALL RELIGIONS ARE ONE

In the adorations and benedictions of righteous men
The praises of all the prophets are kneaded together.
All their praises are mingled into one stream,
All the vessels are emptied into one ewer.
Because He that is praised is, in fact, only One.
In this respect all religions are only one religion.
Because all praises are directed towards God's Light,
These various forms and figures are borrowed from it.

[1] The night of his marriage with Safiyya.

[2] "Form" here is used rather as-soul, the love behind the
     decaying body.

[3] Joseph, a name frequently used by Persian poets, irrespective
     of gender, to symbolise the ideal type of human beauty.

[4] Earthly love.

[5] Koran.

[6] The meaning of this poem is strictly allegorical. We must
     not infer that the All-Good would be a party to the evil
     designs of the Devil. No material gifts, however seductive,
     could succeed in stamping out the Divine Presence in His
     Creatures.

[7] At first sight there seems to be Omarian pessimism in this
     poem. In reality it signifies that all Love is One, which
     shines through the ever-vanishing lanterns of the world.

GHAZALS
OF RUMI

'Why heed the Critics who delight to dart
Their sneer-tipped arrows at translator's art?
The poet's work remains his own at last
Though it in other languages be cast.
And in the sky of Fame it still will shine,
By that which made it at the first divine.
But in this foreign dress some soul may see
A hint of that which fascinated me;
Some deep impression be still deeper made
When by our muse-beloved tongue conveyed;
Some beauty be with newer beauty set;
Some thought that will with fresh emotion fret
Some gentle breast, or with strange music sweep
O'er heaving waters of the spirit's deep.'

Edward Robeson Taylor
of San Francisco.

LIGHT

Until the glorious Sun hath vanquished Night,
The Birds of Day cower trembling with affright.
But lo! a bright glance bids the Tulip ope;
O Heart, awake thou too, in Duty's might.
The Sun's Sword sheds in reddening flush of Dawn
The Blood of Night, and puts the Foe to flight.
The Soul still full of sleep, dreams Night prevails;
But no! Day comes, and triumphs full in sight.
While grey Dawn lingers, dubious yet is Day;
But in Day's glow, who still can doubt the Light.
The Light grows in the East; I in the West
On Mountain top, reflect the Morn's delight.
To Beauty's Sun, I'm but the pale moon here;
Then look from me towards the Sun's face bright.
The Light in East is called Jeláleddín
And here my verse reflects its glowing White.
The Splendour of the Faith.

DEATH AND LIFE

Death endeth sure Life's need and pain;
Yet Life in fear would Death restrain.
Life only sees dark Death's dread Hand,
Not that bright Cup it offered plain.
So shrinks from Love the tender Heart,
As if from threat of being slain.

But when true Love awakens, dies
The Self, that despot dark and vain.
Then let him die in Night's black hour,
And freely breathe in Dawn again.

INVOCATION

Soul of mine, thou dawning Light: Be not far, O be not far!
Love of mine, thou Vision bright: Be not far, O be not far!
Life is where thou smilest sweetly; Death is in thy parting look;
Here mid Death and Life's fierce fight: Be not far, O be not far!
I am East when thou art rising; I am West when thou dost set;
Bring Heaven's own radiant hues to sight: Be not far, O be not far!
See how well my Turban fitteth, yet the Parsee Girdle binds me;
Cord and Wallet I bear light: Be not far, O be not far!
True Parsee and true Brahman, a Christian, yet a Mussulman;
Thee I trust, Supreme by Right: Be not far, O be not far!
In all Mosques, Pagodas, Churches, I do find One Shrine alone;
Thy Face is there my sole delight: Be not far, O be not far!
Thine the World's all-loving Heart; and for it I yearn and pray;
O take not from my Heart thy flight: Be not far, O be not far!
Thee, the World's Eternal Centre, here I circle round in prayer;
Thy absence is last judgment quite: Be not far, O be not far!
Thine, Judgment Day and Blessedness: Mine is Bliss when
Thou art nigh;
Keep me circling in thy Might: Be not far, O be not far!
Fair World Rose, O blossom forth; sweet Heart-buds unfold in Love;
Put on the longing Soul's pure White: Be not far, O be not far!
O Rose, hear through Night's silence, how he thrills—thy Nightingale;
As if I did his Notes indite: Be not far, O be not far!

Jeláleddín, all loving, let Love's Heart resist no more:
Hear him chaunting, Day and Night: Be not far, O be not far!

FAITH

All Unbelief is Midnight, but Faith the Night-Lamp's glow;
Then see that no Thief cometh to steal thy Lamp when low.
Our Hope is for the Sunlight, from which the Lamp did shine;
The Light from which it kindled, still feeds its flame below.
But when the Sun hath risen, both Night and Lamp go out;
And Unbelief and Faith then, the higher Vision know.
O Night! Why art thou dreaming? O Lamp! Why flickerest so?
The swift Sun-horses panting, from East their fire-foam throw.
'Tis Night still in the shadow; the village Lamp burns dim;
But in Dawn's Splendour towering, the Peaks Heaven's
Glory show.

DAWN

The Day has dawned, thy festal Day, O Rose;
Our cheeks all glow in thy bright Ray, O Rose.
Love was the Gardener of the Rose-bed there;
And now thy Flower blooms forth all gay, O Rose.
When Herald Breezes blew: The Rose! the Flowers
Kneeling to thee glad Homage pay, O Rose.
The Tulips danced; the Lilies, drinking there,
Their brightest hues to thee display, O Rose.
The Cypress whispered to the Ivy: Wake!
Why dream'st thou, Child? She dreamed thy Play, O Rose;

The Nightingale a thousand long nights through
But trilled thy own sweet Melody, O Rose.
The Heavens more fair assume thy radiant form,
But thou outviest their Phantasy, O Rose.
The Rose a message brings from Paradise
Where Souls for thee all eager stay, O Rose.
The Rose brings greeting to the Soul from Home;
The Soul forgets thee not for aye, O Rose.
The Rose unfolds the Sign of Beauty there:
God's Seal Himself the Poets say, O Rose.
The Soul crowns all Man's festal Cup of Joy;
That he with thee may breathe Life's May, O Rose.
The Rose is twined in all Life's gladdest Bonds,
That Love from Man ne'er flee away, O Rose.
Be closed in Buds thy Lips; but there let shine
The Smile that ever in thee lay, O Rose.

ALLAH HU!

Sound Drum and mellow Flute, resounding: Allah hu!
Dance, ruddy Dawn, in Gladness bounding: Allah hu!
Sun exalted in the Centre, O thou streaming Light;
Soul of all wheeling Planets rounding: Allah hu!
O Hearts! O Worlds! how soon your Dancing all would stop,
Did not His Power sustain astounding! Allah hu!
Love mazy, winding, changing, all embraces,
The Night, the Dawn, the Day, resounding: Allah hu!
Boom, Sea! on Shore, and Rock, thy Music praising God;
O Nightingale to Rose trill, sounding: Allah hu!
O Soul, what if one Star should falter in the Dance?

His Will is Order ever founding: Allah hu!
Who knows Love's mazy circling, ever lives in God;
For Death, he knows, is Love abounding: Allah hu!
He is God.

SPRING

O Eyes, go forth the Spring to view,
That smiles upon our Plains anew.
A Heavenly Child in cradling Flowers,
Sweet Breath from Skies unclouded drew.
The Morning Breeze his Nurse, that rocked
His Cradle, with soft Lullings due.
The Baby feigns to sleep, and blinks,
Shutting his little Eyelids two.
And when the Lids are oped again,
The Eyebrows drip with sparkling Dew.
The Bees hum round and busy sip
The Nectar, and make Honey new.
O come, and let the Baby's smiles
And Laughter, pierce thee through and through.
O come, and leave your wintry Cell,
And let Heaven's Light thy Life renew.
And build new Cells with honey'd Wax,
Plann'd like the Bees' six-sided, true.
And warmed by radiant Fire of Flowers,
Old Winter's reign of Death undo.
Regret is dead; Love lives again;
New Life transforms the Landscape's Hue.
Bold enter, then, green Spring's loved Haunts,

And drink fresh Wine, nor fear to rue.
And drinking full Love's sweetest Draught,
The glowing Heart new Love shall woo.
Love wakes afresh in Earth and Heaven;
The Rose in green, the Sun in blue.
O Nightingale, behold thy Rose!
O Eagle, thy bright Sun pursue!

SPRING'S FESTIVAL

Our Fasting is over; 'tis Spring's festal Day: Hallelu!
O dearest Guest welcome, all Sorrow's away: Hallelu!
O Love once forsaken, forsaken Heart now be forsaken;
Thy loved One has come, and for ever will stay: Hallelu!
The Parting is parted; the Sev'rance at last is all sever'd;
The Union united, without more delay: Hallelu!
The Flight is now flown off; the Banishment's pain is now banished;
All distant the Distance; our Bird Nest all gay: Hallelu!
The Moon in the Heavens, the Rose in the Heart, in Love's Garden;
The King in his Palace, proud Banners display: Hallelu!
Life stirs in the Rootlet; soft Sap in the Leaflet is spreading;
Green Buds on the Branches are crowning his Sway: Hallelu!
Let come our Foe hated, for now will he meet our Defender;
We scorn and defy him, all safe now for aye: Hallelu!
Yea, flood me all over, all over with Fire of Love burning;
Now well can I bear it; I'll ne'er burn away: Hallelu!
And now it is certain my Soul is bound up in Salvation;
And all of Earth's sadness is sunk in Earth's clay: Hallelu!
O Chalice full brimming, poured out for the thirst of the worlds;
We thank thee, we bless thee, and drink while we pray: Hallelu!

Long parch'd lay the World, a Desert profane, till thy Breath came
On Wings of the Morning, when bright the Dew lay: Hallelu!
We longed as we waited for Spring's Sun our Life to renew;
Jeláleddín's warm Breath from East came to-day: Hallelu!

DEPENDENCE

I am the Vine; Strong Elm, O give me leave,
All round thee my fond Tendrils now to weave.
I am the Ivy; be my Cedar Trunk,
That I no more to Earth's damp soil may cleave.
I am the Bird; O come, be my light Wings,
That soaring I yon azure Heaven retrieve.
I am the Steed; O come and be my spur,
That quick the Victor Goal may me receive.
I am the Rosebud; O be my own Rose,
That gaudy Earth-weeds ne'er my Heart deceive.
I am the East; then rise in me, O Sun,
Flame up in Light, and all my Pain relieve.
I am the Night; O be my Starry Crown,
That in Life's darkness I nor fear, nor grieve.

MYSTICAL UNION

With Thy sweet Soul, this Soul of mine—
Hath mixed as Water doth with Wine.
Who can the Wine and Water part,
Or me and Thee when we combine?

Thou art become my greater Self;
Small Bounds no more can me confine.
Thou hast my Being taken on,
And shall not I now take on Thine?
Me Thou for ever hast affirmed,
That I may ever know Thee mine.
Thy Love has pierced me through and through,
Its Thrill with Bone and Nerve entwine.
I rest a Flute laid on Thy Lips;
A Lute I on Thy Breast recline.
Breathe deep in me that I may sigh;
Yet strike my Strings, and Tears shall shine.
So sweet my Tears, my Sighs so sweet,
I to the World its Joys resign.
Thou restest in my inmost Soul
Whose depths the mirror'd Heaven define.
O Pearl in my Mussel Shell:
O Diamond in my darkest Mine!
My Honey is in Thee dissolved;
O Milk of Life, so mild, so fine!
Our Sweetnesses all blent in Thee,
Give infant Lips their Smiles benign.
Thou crushest me to Drops of Rose;
Nor 'neath the Press do I repine.
In Thy sweet Pain is Pain forgot;
For I, Thy Rose, had this design.
Thou bad'st me blossom on Thy Robe,
And mad'st me for all eyes Thy Sign.
And when Thou pour'st me on the World,
It blows in Beauty, all Divine.

IDENTITY

Although thy Brightness glistens in the Sun, indeed;
Yet is my Light with thine all radiant, One, indeed!
Thou mad'st of Dust all glitt'ring the circling Heavens above;
Yet will with mine thy Spirit ne'er Union shun, indeed!
To Dust return the Heavens; again Heavens spring from Dust;
Yet hast thou in my Being thy own Life spun, indeed!
Now have the Words Eternal that through Heaven's vastness ring,
Found Home in human Bosom, and dearer none, indeed!
Thou hast the Sunbeams hidden, that in the Diamond glow,
Deep, deep in Earth's dark Chambers, a Wonder done, indeed!
See, though in vile Soil feeding, and drinking filthy slime,
To yon Rose peerless Beauty, in Love, hath run, indeed!
O Heart, and be it thou swimmest in Flood, or glow'st in Fire,
The same are Fire and Flood: Be pure, my Son, indeed!
O Mevlana, at Morning I woke, and found with thee,
My Eyes from Tears all brighten'd, and Heaven now won, indeed!

CONFESSION

O Love, to thee I own, I wept in Night's dark Thought;
But now thy radiant Sun to me hath bright Day brought.
O Soul of my own Soul, my I as I am Thou:
Thou art the All, and I in thee have all I sought.
Thou art Life's Sweetness self, Intoxication full,—
The brimming Sea of Pearls, the Gold to pureness wrought.

Whoe'er approaches thee, must first his Soul resign;
He dies beneath thy frown, lives when thy Smile is caught.
Thy Favour thrills in fear the trembling Lover's heart,
Till comes thy Wrath and smites his Weakness into Naught.

DISCORDIA CONCORS

I saw how Sunward soaring, an Eagle cleaved the air;
And how in Shadow sitting, there coo'd a Turtle pair.
I saw how o'er the Heavens, the Clouds in Herds rush'd wild;
And how close round the Shepherd the Lambkins gather'd fair.
I heard the Stars all asking: When shall we rise again?
And Buds in Seedlings folded sigh: Doth Love for us care?
I saw a Grass blade blossom at Morn and fade at Night;
While Cedars braved a thousand Years the Tempests raging there.
I saw old Ocean's Billows like Kings all crowned with foam,
Then flung from Rocks, down fallen, like Penitents in Prayer.
I saw a Dewdrop sparkling, nor did it Danger dread;
But, soon consumed, it vanish'd, that sun-bright Jewel rare.
I saw close crowding Mankind new Towns and Castles rear;
And swarming Ants heaped Hillocks up, with Winter's garner'd fare.
I saw the Warhorse prancing and trampling golden Grain;
And all his Hoofs were redden'd with the Blood of Love's Despair.
I saw the Winter weaving from Flakes a Robe of Death;
And the Spring found Earth in Mourning, all naked, lone and bare.
I heard Time's Loom a-whirring that wove the Sun's dim Veil;
I saw a Worm a-weaving in Life-threads its own Lair.
I saw the Great was Smallest, and saw the Smallest Great;
For God had set His Likeness on all the Things that were.

RENOVATION

Come, O Springtide of my Love: the World, again, make New!
Light in Heaven and Flowers on Earth, o'er Hill and Plain, make New!
With the blue gleaming Sun-gem, set thy new green Turban on;
And o'er the Fields all verdant, thy floral Train, make New!
Paint Meadows fresh with bright Buds, let Hedgerows sprout once
more;
Rose Breast-Knots, slender Lilies in bathing Rain, make New!
Melt with thy warm Breath Winter's iced Coat and frozen Spear;
With tender Smile shame Hatred; Peace, ending Pain, make New!
The Air pines for thy Whisper, and the Rose's Breath is faint;
Then from Slumber rouse thy Zephyrs, and the feather'd Vane,
make New!
Roll, Thunder, pour thy Bounty adown from bursting Cloud;
Now bathe from Head to Foot free, and Death's Disdain, make New!
Strike, Pine, upon the Wind-drum! O Plane-tree, clap thy Hands!
Brooding Love, the dreamy birth Down on feather'd Train, make New!
Vines, twine around the Elm Trees, God's Glory showing fair;
While Violets kiss the soft Sod, Spring's sweet Hymn-strain, make New!
Hyacinths the Tulips fondle; woos Rose the Nightingale.
While Turtles coo in low Notes, my Song's Refrain, make New!
Kindle Altar-fire in Blossoms, in Fragrance Incense burn;
The Pan Pipes that in dead Grass, long have silent lain, make New!
Let Leaves shoot quivering Tongues out, Love's Questionings in Play;
And whisp'ring to each other, Love's Wrangling vain, make New.
Hark! How the Morning Breezes, at rosy Dawn all call:
Up! Up! O Friend, 'tis Spring-time: the Soul's glad Reign, make New!
Behold the Spring in Glory! O thou Alchemist of Flowers,
Smelt the fiery Glow to Blossoms; our World, again, make New!

REVOLVING IN MYSTIC DANCE

Come! Come! Thou art the Soul, the Soul so dear, Revolving!
Come! Come! Thou art the Cedar, the Cedar's Spear, Revolving!
O Come! The Well of Light up-bubbling springs;
And Morning Stars exult, in Gladness sheer, Revolving!
Of the o'er-arching Heavens, the Highest is the Seventh;
But over all thou stretchest, bright, and clear, Revolving!
In warmest Arms of Love thou hold'st me clasped,
And thee I hold enclasped, soft breathing, near, Revolving!
In Sunbeams dance the Motes, by Sunlight grasped,
O Sunlight, grasping me, dispel my Fear, Revolving!
The Motes dance mute, yet telling all of Love;
O silent Love! Teach me thy own Dance here, Revolving!

THE SOUL IN ALL

A mote I in the Sunshine, yet am the Sun's vast Ball;
I bid the Sun spread Sunlight, and make the Mote be small.
I am the Morning Splendour; I am the Evening Breeze;
I am the Leaf's soft Rustle; the Billow's Rise and Fall.
I am the Mast and Rudder, the Steersman and the Ship;
I am the Cliff out-jutting, the Reef of Coral Wall.
I am the Bird Ensnarer, the Bird and Net as well;
I am both Glass and Image; the Echo and the Call.
I am the Tree and Branches, and all the Birds thereon;
I am both Thought and Silence, Tongues' Speech, and Ocean Squall.
I am the Flute when piping, and Man's Soul breathing breath;

I am the sparkling Diamond, and Metals that enthrall.
I am the Grape enclustered, the Wine-press and the Must;
I am the Wine, Cup-bearer, and crystal Goblet tall.
I am the Flame and Butterfly, which round it circling flits;
I am the Rose and Nightingale, the Rose's Passioned Thrall.
I am the Cure and Doctor, Disease and Antidote;
I am the Sweet and Bitter, the Honey and the Gall.
I am the War and Warrior, the Victor and the Field;
I am the City peaceful, the Battle and the Brawl.
I am the Brick and Mortar, the Builder and the Plan,
I am the Base and Gable, new House and ruined Hall.
I am the Stag and Lion, the Lamb and black-maw'd Wolf;
I am the Keeper of them, who shuts them in one Stall.
I am the Chain of Beings, the Ring of circling Worlds;
The Stages of Creation, where'er it rise or fall.
I am what is and is not; I am—O Thou who know'st,
Jeláleddín, O tell it—I AM the Soul in All!

RESPONSIBILITY

O thou who hast come safely, into this Being's Land;
Strange, thou thyself not knowest, how thou didst reach its Strand.—
Straight from the great Shah's Chamber, thou cam'st to Being's Town,
Sent here to do the Business which he himself had planned.
The Lord gave, then, to prove thee, Capacity to do;
And as entrusted Capital, thy Sum of Life in hand.
How has the Market's Turmoil confused thy Sense and Brain;
That thou the Pledge entrusted, can yet not understand?
O cease to dream and rouse thee; and do thy Duty well;
Buy choicest Pearls more wisely, and give not Gold for Sand.
When thou to Home returnest, thou'lt see Him sitting there;

Thy Lord with His Book open, and His own faithful Band.
He will hold count, and reckon all that Himself did give;
And ask how thou did'st use it, when under His Command.
And then will come His Blessing, or Curse, both just and sure,
According as thy Credit, or thy Debt, summed up shall stand.

ACTION

Awake! 'Tis Day! Rise up, O Youthful Mussulman!
Pack quick thy Goods and Baggage, and catch the Caravan.
O List! I hear it coming, 'twill sweep past while you sleep;
Hark! Tinkling Bells are calling to come, while come you can.
When once the Desert Sand-storm has o'er the Foot-prints blown,
You them will find no longer, however close you scan.
Up! Brace yourself for Action, as a Man all prompt and bold;
And waste not Life fond, dreaming, in idlesse, pining, wan.
Think of your noble Forbears, the gallant Youth of old;
Of Rustum, bravest Hero; of Sal, the Pehlevan.
Be, too, of Right the Champion, Knight of the spotless Sun!
Fall not a Prey to Darkness, o'erthrown by Ahriman.
When once in struggle valiant, the earthly Soul is slain,
The Heavenly Soul bears proudly Life's Banner in the Van.
When thou thyself hast conquered, and triumphed in the Fight;
A diamond Ring thou'lt ever shine, in our Lord Shah's Divan.

BONDAGE

Complain not that in Chains, thou here art firmly bound;
Complain not that Earth's Yoke, doth crush thee to the Ground.

Complain not that the World is but a Prison wide;
'Tis only thy complainings that build thy Dungeon round.
And ask not how Life's Riddle will finally unfold;
For soon without thy asking, unfolded 'twill be found.
Say not Love has forsaken or yet forgotten thee;
Love ne'er has Man forsaken; thy Words all falsely sound.
Nor tremble when Death dreaded appears in Terror's Form;
He falls before the Hero, who is with Courage crowned.
Ne'er chase the Phantom, Pleasure; for like a hungry Lion,
'Twill turn and rend in pieces the Hunter most renowned.
Throw not thyself in Fetters; else will Men sternly say:
Complain not of thy Fetters; for thou thyself hast bound.

LOVE'S FREEDOM

O Bird, that freest to Freedom win;
Love caged thee in that Prison thin.
O Soul, if thou, too, wouldst be free,
Then love the Love that shuts thee in.
'Tis Love that twisteth every Snare;
'Tis Love that snaps the Bond of Sin.
Love sounds the Music of the Spheres;
Love echoes through Earth's harshest Din.
Love fills with Fragrance Heaven's sweet Air;
Love's deft Hands Life's gold Fibres spin.
The World is God's pure Mirror clear,
To Eyes when free from Clouds within.
With Love's own Eyes the Mirror view,
And there see God to Self akin.
Then praise Him, Soul, enflamed with Love
As Larks in Dawn, new Songs begin.

IN MY HEART

O, what a Throb of Toil is in my Heart!
What Shrine's crowd-trodden Soil is in my Heart!
The Spring has come; again the Sower sows,
And all the Season's Moil is in my Heart.
The Veil which hid the World's fair face is drawn;
Disclosed, its inmost Coil is in my Heart.
The Heart must higher rise, than setting Suns;
The Sun-dance nought can foil is in my Heart.
The Heart has well been named the Shah's own throne;
And warm anointing Oil is in my Heart.
The Heart's deep Ocean rolls a thousand waves;
And rich Pearl-diver's Spoil is in my Heart.
Jeláleddín! The Heart is sure both Mine and Mint;
For Fire, as Gold did boil, is in my Heart.

NOT DEAF TO LOVE

O Brother hear! Be deaf no more, to Love:
Thy heart now open to its Core, to Love!
Hast thou in Pride, all vain, upraised thy Head?
Come bend it now down to the Floor, to Love.
In Dust thou shalt new living Grace receive,
As Spring awakes the Landscape frore, to Love.
And once thou hast put on Love's Leaves and Flowers,
Comes golden Fruit in Autumn hoar, to Love.
And when thou fadest sere, then burn thyself;
And give thy Ashes, all Earth bore, to Love.

And wing'd, from Ashes wilt thou fairer rise;
And with Love's highest Message soar, to Love.

ASSIMILATION

New Sword from Maker's Hand, in Edge and Point all bright;
See that in dirty Scabbard, it rust not, out of Sight!
Gold that in Miser's Coffer, in Blackness meanly lay,
Upon the Shah's Throne gleaming, becomes a World's Delight.
When full Clouds pour the Rain-drops, lo! every glad Tree drinks;
Fruits redden on the Apple tree, as Leaves grow pale in Fright.
This Stalk an empty Pipe still, in that sweet Sugar swells;
Yet both did sip the same Tank, at Morning, Noon, and Night.
One Deer distils perfumed Musk, another bitterest Gall,
Yet grazed together, side by side, upon the self-same Height.
Two creeping Worms together fed upon the same green Leaf;
One spins mere useless Theadlets, the other Silk aright.
The Bee's Lip, and the Snake's sucked from the self-same Flower;
The one made Honey's Sweetness, the other Poison's Bite.
One dines, and all his Nutriment transmutes to Life divine;
Another's Food is souring to Hatred and to Spite.
One's Eyes drink Light till blinded; the other stores it up,
And glows in rosy Brightness, Love-robed in red and white.
Be pure in all thy Members, and from Nature's golden Tree
Pluck God's own Blessing daily, and grow in Manhood's Might.

CLEANLINESS

Clean be kept thy Garment, and
Clean be kept thy Mouth and Hand.

Clean thy Garment from false Gawds
Clean from all Earth's Filth thy Hand.
Clean thy Heart from earthly Spite;
Clean thy Lips from Greed's Demand.
Outer Threshhold ever clean,
Clean within let all Things stand.
House all clean, might entertain
Angel from the Heavenly Land.
Clean the Food, and clean the cup,
Clean the Wall from smoking Brand.
Son! Thy outward Cleanliness
Pledge of inward is, when scanned.
Clean let Hand and Mouth be kept;
Clean thy Garment's every Strand.

WHERE IS HE?

I ask all I meet: Where is He?
In me incomplete: Where is He?
The Tree of my Thought stretch'd on high,
Reach'd not to His Seat: Where is He?
I ask of the Wanderers by Day:
My loved One, most sweet, Where is He?
I ask of the Keepers of Vines:
My loved One, most sweet, Where is He?
I rush through the Woods and the Fields,
And ask the Stag fleet: Where is He?
At Night when in Darkness He hides,
In Fear I repeat: Where is He?
I ask of the Sun and the Moon,
And Stars in retreat: Where is He?

He is not with me. Who has seen
The Path of His Feet? Where is He?
O Master, if thou hast Him found,
O tell, I entreat: Where is He?

LOVE'S SLAVERY

Come, and be Love's willing Slave;
Thee Love's Slavery will save.
Leave the Slavery of the World,
Take Love's Service, sweet and brave.
The Free, the World makes enslaved;
Aye to Slaves, Love Freedom gave.
As the Bird freed from the Egg,
From the World release I crave.
Free me from the Shell that clings;
Give me Life as from the Grave.
O Love, the Quail in Spring's Free Fields,
In Songs of wildest Joy must rave.

PSYCHE IN TEARS

Psyche sits, and lovelier seems;
Ah! she of her Lover dreams!
Still his Kiss she softly feels;
Still his Smile in Fancy gleams.
But in Light she fain would see
Love's own Self, nor wrong it deems.
Trembling her white Hand hath ta'en

Lamp to light, as Fancy schemes.
There by flickering Flame she scans
Beauty which she Heaven esteems.
But the fluttering Oil did shake,
Shamed to find eclipsed its Beams.
Fell one hot Drop on Love's Hand:
Oh! the Lover waken'd screams!
Love light-pinion'd flies away;
Psyche's Wings, Tears drench in Streams.

SUBSTITUTIONAL

Where the cleansing Water fails,
Sand, as Substitute, avails.
This, at Need, the Prophet gave;
And his Rule to-day prevails.
Know ye, O Believers, why?
Hear the Truth the Sage unveils.—
The Desert oft no Water shows,
But never Sand the Traveller fails.
From the Desert I will guide
Him who me as Leader hails.
To where living Waters flow,
To the Garden Love empales.
Bathe there in Abundance full,
Where no hostile Drought assails.
Full, that Stream Bath, now enjoy'd,
Freedom from Sand Bath entails.
So from Formulas made free,
Spirit Life o'er all prevails.—

Master! Thy high Soul hath seen
Truth through all its hiding Veils

GOD'S THRONE

Unto your Fathers, Allah did make known
This which they handed down and made your own,—
That all who pray My Face may clearly see,
I sit exalted high on Heaven's great Throne.
As I in Heaven, so you I place on Earth,
That I in my Vicegerents, may be shown.
Serve Me then, that the World may serve you too
Made to do good—this is your End alone.
The World was fitly made to help you well:
No Traitors be; let all my Justice own.
And glorify the Maker of the World,
Until the Rose of Peace hath round you blown.

THE LION OF GOD

Fairest Flower beneath the Skies:
Ali Abutaleb's Son!
Fairest Flower in Paradise:
Ali Abutaleb's Son!
God's brave Lion, lamb-like, gentle,
Clearest Mirror, ever bright:
Pure in Faith, without Disguise:
Ali Abutaleb's Son!
Next the Prophet is thy Place,

All his Splendour flashing round:
Thy bright Light too floods our Eyes:
Ali Abutaleb's Son!
By Renouncing, daring Soul,
And by braving Danger too:
Thou hast won the Hero's Prize:
Ali Abutaleb's Son!
Straight thy Strength of Soul and Limb
Bore thee to the thickest Fight:
Death thy giant Thews despise:
Ali Abutaleb's Son!
All the Paths we tread to-day,
Thou hast traced them, Son of Light!
Let on us thy Beams arise:
Ali Abutaleb's Son!
Leader, Guide, and Champion true,
Ever foremost in the Van:
Where thou leadest, Honour lies:
Ali Abutaleb's Son!
Maulānā, in Hymn of Praise
Thee I laud, Jeláleddín!
Even as thou praisest wise,
Ali Abutaleb's Son!

SELF-REALISATION

When I knew myself a Thorn, soft Rose-buds' Swell
I sought for then;
When I saw myself all bitter, sweet Honey's Cell
I sought for then.

When I saw myself all Poison, I quaffed Life's Stream
as Antidote;
When I saw myself Lees turbid, Wine's clear Foam Bell
I sought for then.
When I saw myself all sour Fruit, I caught the ripening
Sunbeams' Glow;
When I saw myself droop feebly, the breezy Fell
I sought for then.
When I saw myself all blinded, the healing Power
of Jesus' Hand;
When I knew it could the Darkness from my Eyes dispel
I sought for then.
Love's Touch became my Eyesalve, and all my Soul's
dull Blindness fled;
And, my Heart of Thirst a-dying, His sweet, pure Well
I sought for then.
I am Fire that never burneth; and thou, the Wind
that makes it burn;
O thou Wind, with my Fire playing, aye in me dwell:
I sought for then.
Rückert avoids the name of Jesus; not so Von Hammer.

THY HAND!

Lord, that I thee may find, O stretch to me thy Hand!
Close-clasped for ever, kind, O stretch to me thy hand!
O'er Earth it gathers dark, and ever deeper here
Where dim cross Footpaths wind, O stretch to me thy
Hand!
The Malice of the World and deadly Hate I know;

Where the Danger grows defined, O stretch to me thy Hand!
The Pilgrim's Journey still is threatened by the Foe;
But to thwart the ill designed, O stretch to me thy Hand!
O come, and let it press upon this burning Heart;
Though Tears my glad Eyes blind, O stretch to me thy Hand!
Fair Moon, up to thy Palace all shining, I would climb;
But lest I halt behind, O stretch to me thy hand!

THE PRIESTS

Love called to Men from Heaven's bright Gate,
'Who look to God now, soon and late?'
''Tis we who look aloft to God,'
To Love replied the Priests elate.
Love cried 'How can ye look on high,
Who thus your Forms and Words inflate?
Ye cannot see where pure Light dwells,
So full your Eyes of Greed and Hate.
Your dark Deeds dim the Noontide's Ray;
Ye shame the Sun while thus ye prate.
The Grace that sits enthroned on high,
Can ne'er its Claim of Faith abate.
Nor can the Just One justly give
The Hearing which ye supplicate.
O ere ye look to Heaven again,
Put off all earthly Pride and State.
Your Hearts let Love, not Hatred, rule;
Then look to God, and on Him wait!'

THE PILGRIMS

The Pilgrims hail the Kaaba's sacred Ground,
When they at last the holy Fane have found.
They see a House of Stone, sublime, revered,
All girt by steep and barren Cliffs around.
They march'd in Hope expecting God to see;
For this they toiled, and still their Prayers abound.
But when all fervent they the Threshold tread,
They hear a voice from out the Temple sound:
'Why pray ye thus, O Fools, to Clay and Stone?
Revere the House for which the Pure are bound.
The Heart's own House, Shrine of the True, the One:
O blest are they whose Striving there is crown'd!
Blest those who tread no Desert's weary Way,
But rest at Home in peace, like Shems renown'd.'

MANY FAITHS, ONE LORD

Our House has many Doors indeed,
But all to One Lord inward lead.
And all who reach this Lord must pray,
With Forehead on the Ground, and plead.
And many in the House born blind,
The Lord's commands yet hear and heed.
The Lame there too can Service give,
They all perform House Tasks at need.
Yea, even the Wind with panting Breath,
Comes in, the Hearth's low Fire to feed.

Each one must do his Part as bid,
No one can choose his Share or Deed.
Yet many deem them free, nor know
The Bond that binds them firm decreed.
But if thou humbly bear thy Bond,
It holds a Crown of Flowers in Seed.
Plight Troth, and Grace will answer Sure,
For Love's Vow seals the highest Creed.
Servant! To Fellow-servants shew
The lowly Mien no Hate will breed.
Forbearing be! Thy Over-Lord
No Pleasure hath in Pride or Greed.
Can one e'er claim to enter bold
Who Entrance never would concede?
Who dares to haggle with the Master,
He drives them from His Doors with Speed.

LOVE ABSOLUTE

Love lies not in Book, or Letter, or well reason'd Tome—O no!
Love lives not in Cell of Penance, nor in gloomy Home—O no!
From the Green of Spring eternal shoots up the Tree of Life;
Yet Milkyway and Pleiad reach not Love's Dome—O no!
Reason dismounts before her, Desire her Charioteer;
So long the Way no slower to Love's Realm would come—O no!
While thou art still a Lover, the Longing in thee moves;
But when thou art the Loved One, thou need'st not roam—O no!
Wrecked Landsmen shriek in Terror, though saving spars float round;
The Pilot steeped in rapture, recks not Death's Foam—O no!
Jeláleddín, thy soul in Ocean melts in joy:
Thyself all Consecration, no Novice far from Home—O no!

RENUNCIATION

Since he to me his loving Heart has shown,
I give my Life to him, as All his own.
The Body's House becomes his Temple now,
Until the Soul herself to Heav'n hath flown.
The Earthly Life is Offering far too small;
Then let the Eternal, silent All atone.
Jeláleddín in self-negation found
The Rose of Life divinely fair, full blown.

ALL FULNESS

Ever shall I more desire
Than Time's bounded Needs require.
Ever as more Flowers I pluck,
Blossoms new gay Spring attire.
And when through the Heavens I sweep,
Rolling Spheres will flash new Fire.
Perfect Beauty only can
True Eternal Love inspire.

FRIENDSHIP

The Rose is aye Love's dearest, sweetest Sign;
To my Friend's Heart, I give this Rose of mine.

Clear Thought dies out in Love's absorbed Delight,
As Weeds grow pale before the Rose and pine.
The Rose hides in her Heart the piercing Thorn,
For deepest hidden Pains with Love entwine.
The Rose is Beauty perfected in One,
Her Charms all glowing, Heaven and Earth outshine.
The full blown Rose in Splendour dims the Sun;
Each quivering Leaflet shows a Moon's design.
The Sun's sphered Light is moulded in her Form,
While bright-eyed Stars keep watch around her
Shrine.
O Sun, the Rose that made the Moon to grow,
To my Heart's Friend give Love and Joy divine!

THE FRIEND SUPREME

O what a Friend is mine!
O what a burning Flame!
My Heart was parched and dead,
Till His Breath o'er me came.
When I before Him fled,
By Love's Keen Pang distressed;
He cried, Why dost thou flee?
Thou art thyself to blame.
At Night I asked the Moon,
Where hid my Moon still stayed?
She said, My Cheek grew pale,
In Fear when told His Name.
The Sun, when risen, I asked,
And why art thou so dim?

He said, My Eyelids dull
In Tears have veil'd their Shame.
And to the Sea I said,
Why canst thou not be still?
She answer'd, Deep Unrest
Will leave me ne'er the Same.
I cried to Fire, Flame Queen:
Why flickerest thou So?
On me, she cried, He looked,
And quench'd all Earthly Aim.
I shouted then, O Wind:
Why hurriest to and fro?
She gasped, His Breath consumes me,
Whene'er my Pace I tame!
But what in me, too, meaneth
This elemental Strife?
The Cup in my Hand shaketh,
And Fever thrills my Frame.
In Revel's Glow enraptured,
His Love I know my own:
Then, come, pour foaming Wine out,
Till o'er All flows His Name.

IMMORTALITY

I am the Bird of Paradise;
And still my Nest is in the Skies.
I am the Spirit Falcon, flown
From Heav'n's Tent, where it open lies.
But in my eager Chase of Prey,

I fell to where new Sense Worlds rise.
I am the Hero of Mount Kaf,
Who braves the Death the Weakling flies.
I look on high, until he call
Me home from this far Enterprise.
I look up steadfast, searching keen,
Until my Gaze the Throne descries.
There all secure my Nest bides near
The Tree of Life, where Nothing dies.

THE FIRST AND LAST

Thou art of all Man's Joys the Spring;
Life's honey'd Sweetness thou dost bring.
My gather'd Pearls, from Bosom full,
Before thy Feet my glad Hands fling.
The Souls love-moved, are circling on,
Like Streams to their great Ocean King.
Thou art the Sun of all Men's Thoughts;
Thy Kisses are the Flowers of Spring.
The Dawn is pale from yearning Love;
The Moon in Tears is sorrowing.
Thou art the Rose; and deep for thee,
In Sighs, the Nightingales still sing.
O can my Love me so despise,
That he my Heart with Pain can wring?
O Wine of Life, all fragrant, pour,
And soothe the Pain of Death's last Sting!

MYSTIC LOVE DANCE

On with the Dance! We fly upon the Wings of Love;
We glow in all the Joys and scorn the Stings of Love.
I heard Love joyous calling from out the Realm of Death;
Lo! God hath drown'd dark Death now in living Springs
of Love.
The Power of Life that loosen'd my Band when I was born,
That Hour my Mother gave me the Leading Strings of Love.
I asked Love's Self, fond nursing: How shall I Love escape?
She said: There is no Outlet from encircling Rings of Love.
Love's magic Mirror radiates a Thousand Worlds most fair;
And wondering Eyes look dazzled on all it brings of Love.
Thy Body's gold surrender to Love's refining Flames,
The Gold is Dross till boiling, all pure, it sings of Love.
I tell thee why the Ocean aye tosses glittering Spray:
It dances and it glances with Gems, Playthings of Love.
I tell thee how was Mankind a-formed from Earthy Dust:
God in the Dust inbreathèd sweet Whisperings of Love.
I tell thee why the Heavens for ever circle round:
God's Throne set in the Centre, draws All on Wings
of Love.
I tell thee why the Zephyr at Morn so softly blows:
To flutter every Leaflet with the Kiss it flings of Love.
I tell thee why Night hideth in Veil so dark her Face:
She makes the World a bridal Tent, and darkling sings
of Love.
I can divine all Riddles Creation puts to me,
For to her Riddles Ever, Man the Answer brings of Love.

DREAM FEAR

O Love, the Realm of Dreams
Is thine; they come, unsought:
With fiery Weapons, throng'd,
As if whole Armies fought.
The Standard of thy Rule,
Hot Hearts bear in the Van;
It flames till Worlds, o'ercome,
Beneath thy Sway are brought.
Thou, ever and again,
Sendst out a Phantom Form;
Till cower weak, trembling Souls,
Like Children terror-wrought.
But when a Soul resigns,
Thou, Victor, marchest in:
A Conqueror—lovelier far
Than ever Soul had thought.

THE CRY OF LOVE

My Soul sends up to Heaven each Night the Cry of Love!
Hu! Hu!
God's starry Beauty draws with Might the Cry of Love!
Hu! Ya!
Bright Sun and Moon each Morn dance in my Heart at
Dawn;
And waking me in Daylight, excite the Cry of Love!

On every Meadow glancing, I see God's Sunbeams play;
And all Creation's Wonders incite the Cry of Love!
The Turtledove embowered, awakened by my Call,
Returns to me in coo'd Delight, the Cry of Love!
Gu! Gu!
The Crag on whose bare Forehead thy Light in Glory falls,
Resounds in Echoes clear, aright the Cry of Love!
Men! Hu!
For all the Flowers sweet blowing in timid Silence there,
For deaf Worms, too, I offer God's Rite, the Cry of Love!
The Ocean's speechless Billows sound ever loud thy Praise;
And all in rolling Anthems recite the Cry of Love!
To thee for every Rosebud and every Dewdrop fair,
And every Gem, deep hidden, I plight the Cry of Love!
Hu! Ya!
I, All in All becoming, now clear see God in All;
And up for Union yearning, takes Flight the Cry of Love!
Hu! Hu!

NIGHT THOUGHT

Sleep not, O Thought, my Guest—the livelong Night!
I bring thee Friendship's best—the livelong Night!
Thou, like an Angel's Breath, from Heaven hast come,
To heal me while I rest—the livelong Night!
Banish dull Slumber, let Heaven's Mystery sing,
From out his secret Nest—the livelong Night!
Shine clear, ye circling Stars, that in your Rays,
The Soul its Vision test—the livelong Night!
Ye Diamonds, sparkling in your dark Retreats,

Rival the starry West—the livelong Night!
Soar up, O Eagle, Sunwards—higher, higher!
Be still thy Flight up pressed—the livelong Night!
Thank God, the World now sleeps; alone are God
And I, all God-possess'd—the livelong Night!
The Night is calm and deep, and Heaven's own Lyre,
Sounds soft, as Star-caress'd—the livelong Night!
War's Turmoil whirling through the starry Streets,
New spheral Choirs attest—the livelong Night!
With Lion, Bull, and Ram, all warlike gleam
Orion's Sword and Crest—the livelong Night!
Scorpion and Dragon seize the Crown, while weeps
The Virgin sore opprest—the livelong Night!
My Tongue sinks dumb with rapture, drunk with Love;
Now, Thought, brood, silent, blest—the live long Night!

UP OUT OF NIGHT

O for Wings to Heaven to soar—
Up out of Night!
A Heart to Struggle to Light's Shore—
Up out of Night!
Lo! How God's Messengers of Love,
In dancing Dawn:
In Life and Light new Worlds restore,
Up out of Night!
See in the West how Daylight there,
Slow Sinking down:
Looks back, with Love all blushing sore,
Up out of Night!
And now in East where she again,

Doth rise all fair;
Blooms Rose Dawn, brightening as of yore,
Up out of Night!
Time's Memories clear and Life's bright Hopes
Together twine:
Hands loving stretch to us once more,
Up out of Night!
The Eternal Stars all sparkling ope
Their radiant Eyes;
And flash anew deep Wisdom's Lore,
Up out of Night!
And ere Heavens full-blown Rose shall fade,
The endless Day
Shall rise in Bliss at thy Heart's Core,
Up out of Night!
O Nightingale that woos for aye
The Heavenly Rose:
Now, now thy deepest Love Notes pour,
Up out of Night!

ALL ONE

I looked around, and saw in all Heaven's Spaces: One!
In Ocean's rippling Waves and billowy Races: One!
I looked into the Heart, and saw a Sea, wide Worlds
All full of Dreams, and in all Dreaming Faces: One!
Thou art the First, the Last, the Outer, Inner, Whole:
Thy Light breaks through in all Earth's Hues and Graces: One!
Thou seest All from East to furthest Bound of West,
And lo! each Leaf and Flower and Tree Crown traces: One!
Four wild and restive Steeds draw on the World's vast Car;

Thou bridlest them, and rul'st in all their Paces: One!
Air, Fire, Earth, Water melt to One in Fear of thee;
Nor struggle wild, but show in close Embraces: One!
The Hearts of all that live in Earth and Heav'n above,
Beat Praise to thee; nor fails in all their Places—One.

O WAKE IN ME

When all the World has gone to rest,
O Wake in Me!
When tired Eyes close by Sleep opprest,
O Wake in Me!
When Eyes in Heaven all sleepless watch
with Starry gaze,
Make my blind Orbs thy Home as Guest,
O Wake in Me!
When all my outer Gates of Sense,
are shut and bar'd;
Lest, lone, my Soul be fear-possest,
O Wake in Me!
That no grim Power of Darkness through
the Gloom around,
My deeper Peace and Calm molest,
O Wake in Me!
From Eden's Garden still soft blown,
That fragrant Air
The healing Tree of Life attest,
O Wake in Me!
That once, at least in Dream, Life's Good
be here attained,

The Heart no more by pain distrest,
O Wake in Me!
In the moist Midnight dank and drear,
where Shadows creep,
Lest Passions vile my Heart infest,
O Wake in Me!
And when Life's Night is gone, and Love's
new dawning Smile
Woos me for ever to thy Breast,
O Wake in Me!

JELÁLEDDÍN

Highest Love, where thou art thronèd, here before Thy Throne unseen,
O let me pour my Melodies, my sweetest, highest yet, I ween.
If well-pleasing they ascending reach Thine ear in tones of power,
All their work of soul-subduing comes from Thy own soul serene.
Let them hymn and let them praise thee: let them cry and supplicate:
Where is he to Earth descended, Star from out thy Glory's Sheen?
He his Head with thy soft Roses wreathed, and struck the charmèd String,
Till drunk with Love he passed sweet playing to the Light no cloud
can screen.
He beclad in Garments waving here on broken Pillar leaned,
Pouring Songs by which upwafted he hath left this lower Scene.
Hath he now flown to Thy Bosom? Tell me, Love, who here below
Didst his Soul so sweetly cherish, where still cherished hath he been?—
Where the Peoples sink their Banners, where Pride lays her Signs aside,
All their Caste Distinctions blending, where eternal Peace is Queen.
There among the Saints, the purest, of all Zones, is he now found:
Hail! All hail his Memory holy: Maulānā Jelál-ed-Dín!

SELECTIONS
FROM THE DĪVĀNI
SHAMSI TABRĪZ

I AM SILENT

I am silent. Speak Thou, O Soul of Soul of Soul,
From desire of whose Face every atom grew articulate.

A CRY TO
THE BELOVED

Yestereve I delivered to a star tidings for thee:
"Present," I said, "my service to that moon-like form."
I bowed, I said: "Bear that service to the sun
Who maketh hard rocks gold by his burning."
I bared my breast, I showed it the wounds:
"Give news of me," I said, "to the Beloved whose drink
is blood."
I rocked to and fro that the child, my heart, might become still;
A child sleeps when one sways the cradle.
Give my heart-babe milk, relieve us from its weeping,
O Thou that helpest every moment a hundred helpless
like me.
The heart's home, first to last, is Thy City of Union:
How long wilt Thou keep in exile this heart forlorn?

REMEMBER GOD AND FORGET SELF

O spirit, make thy head in search and seeking like the water
of a stream,
And O reason, to gain Eternal Life tread ever-lastingly the way
of Death.
Keep God in remembrance till self is forgotten,
That thou may be lost in the Called, without distraction of
caller and call.

THE PRINCE OF THE FAIR

A garden—may its rose be in flower to Resurrection!
An idol—may the two worlds be scattered o'er his beauty!
The Prince of the Fair goes proudly forth to the chase at morning;
May our hearts fall a prey to the arrow of His glance
From His eye what messages are passing continually to mine!
May my eyes be gladdened and filled with intoxication by
His Message!

MY BODY IS LIKE THE MOON

My body is like the moon which is melting for Love,
My heart like Zuhra's lute—may its strings be broken!
Look not on the moon's waning nor on Zuhra's broken state:
Behold the sweetness of his affection—may it wax a thousandfold!

MORTALITY AND IMMORTALITY

What a Bride is in the soul! By the reflection of Her face
May the world be freshened and coloured like the hands of the
newly married!
Look not on the fleshy cheek which corrupts and decays,
Look on the spiritual cheek—may it be sweet and agreeable!
The dark body resembles a raven, and the body's world winter;
O in spite of these two unpleasants may there be Eternal Spring!

THE BELOVED THE DIVINE CONSOLER

Thou who art my soul's comfort in the season of sorrow,
Thou who art my spirit's treasure in the bitterness of dearth!
That which the imagination has not conceived, that which the
understanding has not seen,
Visited my soul from Thee; hence in worship I turn toward Thee.
By Thy grace I keep fixed on Eternity my amorous gaze,
Except, O King, the pomps that perish lead me astray.
The favour of that one, who brings glad tidings of Thee,
Even without Thy summons, is sweeter in mine ear than songs.

* * * * *

If a never-ceasing bounty should offer kingdoms,
If a hidden treasure should set before me all that is,
I would bend down my soul, I would lay my face in the dust,
I would say, "Of all these the love of such an One for me!"

107

THOU ART THE SOUL OF THE WORLD

Eternal Life, methinks, is the time of Union,
Because Time, for me, hath no place There.
Life is the vessels, Union the clear draught in them;
Without Thee what does the pain of the vessels avail me?
I had twenty thousand desires ere this;
In passion for Him not even (care of) my safety remained.
By the help of His grace I am become safe, because
The unseen King saith to me, "Thou art the soul of the world."

THE VOICE OF LOVE

Every moment the voice of Love is coming from left and right.
We are bound for heaven: who has a mind to sight-seeing?
We have been in heaven, we have been friends of the angels;
Thither, Sire, let us return, for that is our country.

THE SEA OF LOVE

Mankind, like waterfowl, are sprung from the sea—the Sea of Soul;
Risen from that Sea, why should the bird make here his home?
Nay, we are pearls in that Sea, therein we all abide;
Else, why does wave follow wave from the Sea of Soul?
'Tis the time of Union's attainment, 'tis the time of Eternity's beauty,
'Tis the time of favour and largesse, 'tis the Ocean of perfect purity.

The billow of largesse hath appeared, the thunder of the Sea hath
arrived,
The morn of blessedness hath dawned. Morn? No, 'tis the Light
of God.

THE BEAUTY OF THE BELOVED

O Beloved, spiritual beauty is very fair and glorious,
But Thine own beauty and loveliness is another thing.
O Thou who art years describing Spirit,
Show one quality that is equal to His Essence.
Light waxes in the eye at the imagination of Him,
But in presence of His Union it is dimmed.
I stand open-mouthed in veneration of that beauty:
"God is most great" is on my heart's lips every moment.
The heart hath gotten an eye constant in desire of Thee.
O how that desire feeds heart and eye!
'Tis slave-caressing Thy Love has practised;
Else, where is the heart worthy of that Love?
Every heart that has slept one night in Thy air
Is like radiant day.

THE WATER OF ETERNAL LIFE

Every form you see has its archetype in the placeless world;
If the form perished, no matter, since its Original is everlasting.
Every fair shape you have seen, every deep saying you have heard,
Be not cast down that it perished; for that is not so.
Whereas the Spring-head is undying, its branch gives water continually;

Since neither can cease, why are you lamenting?
Conceive the Soul as a fountain, and these created things as rivers:
While the Fountain flows, the rivers run from it.
Put grief out of your head and keep quaffing this River-water;
Do not think of the Water failing, for this Water is without end.

EARTHLY LOVE AND THE
LOVE DIVINE

'Twere better that the spirit which wears not true Love as a garment
Had not been: its being is but shame.

* * * * *

Without the dealing of Love there is no entrance to the Beloved.

* * * * *

'Tis Love and the Lover that live to all Eternity;
Set not thy heart on aught else; 'tis only borrowed,
How long wilt thou embrace a dead beloved?
Embrace the Soul which is embraced by nothing.
What was born of spring dies in autumn,
Love's rose-plot hath no aiding from the early spring.

THE HOUSE OF LOVE

This is the Lord of Heaven, who resembles Venus and the moon,
This is the House of Love, which has no bound or end.

Like a mirror, the soul has received Thy image in its heart;
The tip of Thy curl has sunk into my heart like a comb.
Forasmuch as the women cut their hands in Joseph's presence,
Come to me, O soul, for the Beloved is in the midst.

LOVE'S DESIRE

Show Thy face, for I desire the orchard and the rose-garden;
Ope Thy lips, for I desire sugar in plenty.
O sun, show forth Thy face from the veil of cloud,
For I desire that radiant glowing countenance.

THE FINDING OF THE BELOVED

I was on that day when the Names were not,
Nor any sign of existence endowed with name,
By me Names and Named were brought to view
On the day when there was not "I" and "We,"
For a sign, the tip of the Beloved's curl became a centre
of revelation;
As yet the tip of that curl was not.
Cross and Christians, from end to end,
I surveyed; He was not on the Cross.
I went to the idol-temple, to the ancient pagoda;
No trace was visible there.
I went to the mountains of Herāt and Candahār;
I looked; He was not in that hill-and-dale.

* * * * *

111

I gazed into my own heart;
There I saw Him; He was nowhere else.

GOD ONLY

"None but God has contemplated the beauty of God."
This eye and that lamp are two lights, each individual,
When they came together, no one distinguished them.

THE MOON-SOUL
AND THE SEA

At morning-tide a moon appeared in the sky,
And descended from the sky and gazed on me.
Like a falcon which snatches a bird at the time of hunting,
That moon snatched me up and coursed over the sky.
When I looked at myself, I saw myself no more,
Because in that moon my body became by grace even as soul.
When I travelled in soul, I saw naught save the moon,
Till the secret of the Eternal Theophany was revealed.
The nine spheres of heaven were all merged in that moon,
The vessel of my being was completely hidden in the sea.
The sea broke into waves, and again Wisdom rose
And cast abroad a voice; so it happened and thus it befell.
Foamed the sea, and at every foam-fleck
Something took figure and something was bodied forth.
Every foam-fleck of body, which received a sign from that sea,
Melted straightway and turned to spirit in this Ocean.

LIFE IN DEATH

When my bier moveth on the day of Death,
Think not my heart is in this world.
Do not weep in the devil's snare: that is woe.
When thou seest my hearse, cry not "Parted, parted!"
Union and meeting are mine in that hour.
If thou commit me to the grave, say not "Farewell, farewell!"
For the grave is a curtain hiding the communion of Paradise,
After beholding descent, consider resurrection;
Why should setting be injurious to the sun and moon?
To thee it seems a setting, but 'tis a rising;
Tho' the vault seems a prison, 'tis the release of the soul.

* * * * *

Shut thy mouth on this side and open it beyond,
For in placeless air will be thy triumphal song.

THE WHOLE AND
THE PART

Beware! do not keep, in a circle of reprobates,
Thine eye shut like a bud, thy mouth open like the rose.
The world resembles a mirror: thy Love is the perfect image:
O people, who has ever seen a part greater than the whole?

THE DIVINE FRIEND

Look on me, for thou art my companion in the grave
On the night when thou shalt pass from shop and dwelling.
Thou shalt hear my hail in the hollow of the tomb: it shall
become known to thee
That thou wast never concealed from mine eye.
I am as reason and intellect within thy bosom
At the time of joy and gladness, at the time of sorrow
and distress.

*****

In the hour when the intellectual lamp is lighted,
What a pears goes up from the dead men in the tombs!

ASPIRATION

Haste, haste! for we too, O soul, are coming
From this world of severance to that world of Union.
O how long shall we, like children, in the earthly sphere
Fill our lap with dust and stones and sherds?
Let us give up the earth and fly heavenwards,
Let us flee from childhood to the banquet of men.
Behold how the earthly frame has entrapped thee!
Rend the sack and raise thy head clear.

I WELL CHERISH THE SOUL

"I am a painter, a maker of pictures; every moment I shape
a beauteous form,
And then in Thy presence I melt them all away.
I call up a hundred phantoms and indue them with a spirit;
When I behold Thy phantom, I cast them in the fire."

* * * * *

Lo! I will cherish the soul, because it has a perfume of Thee.
Every drop of blood which proceeds from me is saying to
Thy dust:
"I am one colour with Thy love, I am a partner of Thy affection."
In the house of water and clay this heart is desolate
without Thee;
O Beloved, enter the house, or I will leave it.

THIS IS LOVE

This is Love: to fly heavenward,
To rend, every instant, a hundred veils.
The first moment, to renounce Life:
The last step, to feel without feet.
To regard this world as invisible,
Not to see what appears to one's self.
"O heart," I said, "may it bless thee
To have entered the circle of lovers,

115

To look beyond the range of the eye,
To penetrate the windings of the bosom!
Whence did this breath come to thee, O my soul,
Whence this throbbing, O my heart?"

THE JOURNEY TO THE BELOVED

O lovers, O lovers, it is time to abandon the world:
The drum of departure reaches my spiritual ear from heaven.
Behold, the driver has risen and made ready his files of camels,
And begged us to acquit him of blame: why, O travellers,
are you asleep?
These sounds before and behind are the din of departure
and of the camel-bells;
With each moment a soul and spirit is setting off into the
Void.
From these inverted candles, from these blue awnings
There has come forth a wondrous people, that the
mysteries may be revealed.
A heavy slumber fell upon thee from the circling spheres:
Alas, for this life so light, beware of this slumber so heavy!
O soul, seek the Beloved, O friend, seek the Friend,
O watchman, be wakeful: it behoves not a watchman to sleep.

THE DAY OF RESURRECTION

On every side is clamour and tumult, in every street are
candles and torches,

For to-night the teeming world gives birth to the World Everlasting.

Thou wert dust and art spirit, thou wert ignorant and art wise.

He who has led thee thus far will lead thee further also.

How pleasant are the pains He makes thee suffer while He gently draws thee to Himself!

THE RETURN OF THE BELOVED

Always at night returns the Beloved: do not eat opium to-night;

Close your mouth against food, that you may taste the sweetness of the mouth.

Lo, the cup-bearer is no tyrant, and in his assembly there is a circle:

Come into the circle, be seated; how long will you regard the revolution (of Time)?

* * * * * *

Why, when God's earth is so wide, have you fallen asleep in a prison?

Avoid entangled thoughts, that you may see the explanation of Paradise.

Refrain from speaking, that you may win speech hereafter.

Abandon life and the world, that you may behold the Life of the world.

THE CALL OF THE BELOVED

Every morning a voice comes to thee from heaven:
"When thou lay'st the dust of the way, thou win'st thy way
to the goal."
On the road to the Ka'ba of Union, lo, in every thorn-bush
Are thousands slain of desire who manfully yielded up their lives.
Thousands sank wounded on this path, to whom there came not
A breath of the fragrance of Union, a token from the
neighbourhood of the Friend.

"THE BANQUET OF UNION"

In memory of the banquet of Union, in yearning for His beauty
They are fallen bewildered by the wine Thou knowest.
How sweet, in the hope of Him, on the threshold of His Abode,
For the sake of seeing His face, to bring night round to day!
Illumine thy bodily senses by the Light of the soul:

* * * * *

Look not in the world for bliss and fortune, since thou wilt
not find them;
Seek bliss in both worlds by serving Him,
Put away the tale of Love that travellers tell;
Do thou serve God with all thy might.

"BE SILENT"

Be silent that the Lord who gave thee language may speak,
For as He fashioned a door and lock, He has also made a key.

"THOU DIDST
GO TO THE ROSE-GARDEN"

At last thou hast departed and gone to the Unseen;
'Tis marvellous by what way thou wentest from the world.
Thou didst strongly shake thy wings and feathers, and having
broken thy cage
Didst take to the air and journey towards the world of Soul.
Thou wert a favourite falcon, kept in captivity by an old woman:
When thou heard'st the falcon-drum thou didst fly away into
the Void.
Thou wert a love-lorn nightingale among owls:
The scent of the Rose-Garden, reached thee, and thou didst
go to the Rose-Garden.

"THE WORLD GAVE THEE FALSE CLUES"

The world gave thee false clues, like a ghoul:
Thou took'st no heed of the clue, but wentest to that which
is without a clue.
Since thou art now the sun, why dost thou wear a tiara?

Why seek a girdle, since thou art gone from the middle?
I have heard that thou art gazing with distorted eyes upon thy soul:
Why dost thou gaze on thy soul, since thou art gone to the Soul
of soul?
O heart, what a wondrous bird art thou, that in chase of divine
rewards
Thou didst fly with two wings to the spear-point, like a shield!
The rose flees from autumn—O what a fearless rose art thou,
Who didst go loitering along in the presence of the autumn wind!
Falling like rain from heaven upon the roof of the terrestrial world
Thou didst run in every direction till thou didst escape by conduit.
Be silent and free from the pain of speech: do not slumber,
Since thou hast taken refuge with so loving a Friend.

"HE COMES"

He comes, a moon whose like the sky ne'er saw, awake or dreaming,
Crowned with Eternal Flame no flood can lay.
Lo, from the flagon of Thy Love, O Lord, my soul is swimming,
And ruined all my body's house of clay!
When first the Giver of the grape my lonely heart befriended,
Wine fired my bosom and my veins filled up,
But when His image all mine eye possessed, a voice descended:
"Well done, O sovereign Wine and peerless Cup!"
Love's mighty arm from roof to base each dark abode is hewing
Where chinks reluctant catch a golden ray.
My heart, when Love's sea of a sudden burst into its viewing,
Leaped headlong in, with "Find me now who may!"

"THE ROAD BE THINE TOWARDS
THE SHRINE"

O honoured guest in Love's high feast, O bird of the angel-sphere,
'Tis cause to weep, if thou wilt keep thy habitation here.
A voice at morn to thee is borne—God whispers to the soul—
"If on the way the dust thou lay, thou soon wilt gain the goal."
The road be thine toward the Shrine! and lo, in bush and briar,
The many slain of Love and pain in flower of young desire,
Who on the track fell wounded back and saw not, ere the end,
A ray of bliss, a touch, a kiss, a token of the Friend!

THY ROSE

Our Sweetnesses all bleat in Thee,
Give infant lips their smiles benign.
Thou crushest me to drops of Rose
Nor 'neath the press do I repine.
In Thy sweet Pain is pain forgot;
For I, Thy Rose, had this design.
Thou bad'st me blossom on Thy Robe,
And mad'st me for all eyes Thy sign.
And when Thou pour'st me on the world,
It blows in beauty, all Divine.

"I SAW THE WINTER WEAVING"

I saw the winter weaving from flakes a robe of Death;
And the spring found earth in mourning, all naked, lone, and bare.
I heard Time's loom a-whirring that wove the Sun's dim Veil;
I saw a worm a-weaving in Life-threads its own lair.
I saw the Great was Smallest, and saw the Smallest Great;
For God had set His likeness on all the things that were.

LOVE SOUNDS
THE MUSIC OF THE SPHERES

O, soul, if thou, too, wouldst be free,
Then love the Love that shuts thee in.
'Tis Love that twisteth every snare;
'Tis Love that snaps the bond of sin;
Love sounds the Music of the Spheres;
Love echoes through Earth's harshest din.

* * * * *

The world is God's pure mirror clear,
To eyes when free from clouds within.
With Love's own eyes the Mirror view,
And there see God to self akin.

122

THE SOULS LOVE-MOVED

The souls love-moved are circling on,
Like streams to their great Ocean King.
Thou art the Sun of all men's thoughts;
Thy kisses are the flowers of spring.
The dawn is pale from yearning Love;
The moon in tears is sorrowing.
Thou art the Rose, and deep for Thee,
In sighs, the nightingales still sing.

THE BELOVED ALL
IN ALL

My Soul sends up to Heaven each night the cry of Love!
God's starry Beauty draws with might the cry of Love!
Bright sun and moon each morn dance in my Heart at Dawn:
And waking me at daylight, excite the cry of Love!
On every meadow glancing, I see God's sun-beams play;
And all Creation's wonders excite the cry of Love!

* * * * *

I, All in All becoming, now clear see God in All;
And up from Union yearning, takes flight the cry of Love!

THOU AND I

Happy the moment when we are seated in the Palace, thou and I,
With two forms and with two figures but with one soul, thou
and I.
The colours of the grove and the voice of the birds will bestow
immortality
At the time when we come into the garden, thou and I.
The stars of heaven will come to gaze upon us;
We shall show them the moon itself, thou and I.
Thou and I, individuals no more, shall be mingled in ecstasy,
Joyful, and secure from foolish babble, thou and I.
All the bright-plumed birds of heaven will devour their hearts
with envy
In the place where we shall laugh in such a fashion, thou and I.
This is the greatest wonder, that thou and I, sitting here in the
same nook,
Are at this moment both in Irāq and Khorasan, thou and I.

SELECTED
ANECDOTES FROM
MENĀQIBU 'L 'ĀRIFĪN

THE ACTS OF THE ADEPTS

CHAPTER I

Bahá'u-'d-Dīn, Veled, Sultānu-'l-'Ulemā (The Beauty of the Religion of Islām, Son, Sultan of the Doctors of the Law).

1

The king of Khurāsān, 'Alā'u-'d-Dīn Muhammed, Khurrem-Shāh, uncle of Jelālu-'d-Dīn Muhammed Kh'ārezm-Shāh, and the proudest, as he was the most handsome man of his time, gave his daughter, Melika'i-Jihān (Queen of the World), as to the only man worthy of her, to Jelālu-'d-Dīn Huseyn, el Khatībī, of the race of Abū-Bekr.

An ancestor of his was one of the original Muslim conquerors of Khurāsān. He was himself very virtuous and learned, surrounded with numerous disciples. He had not married until then; which gave him many an anxious and self-accusing thought.

He himself, the king, the king's daughter, and the king's Vazīr were all four warned in a dream by the Prince of the Apostles of

God (Muhammed) that he should wed the princess; which was done. He was then thirty years old. In due course, nine months afterwards, a son was born to him, and was named Bahā'u-'d-Dīn Muhammed. He is commonly mentioned as Bahā'u-'d-Dīn Veled.

When adolescent, this latter was so extremely learned that the family of his mother wished to raise him to the throne as king; but this he utterly rejected.

By the divine command, as conveyed in the selfsame night, and in an identical dream, to three hundred of the most learned men of the city of Balkh, the capital of the kingdom, where he dwelt, those sage doctors unanimously conferred upon him the honorific title of Sultānu-'l-'Ulemā, and they all became his disciples.

Such are the names and titles by which he is more commonly mentioned; but he is also styled Mevlānāyi Buzurg (the Greater or Elder Master). Many miracles and prodigies were attributed to him; and some men were found who conceived a jealousy at his growing reputation and influence.

2

In A.H. 605 (A.D. 1208) he, Bahā'u-'d-Dīn Veled, began to preach against the innovations of the king and sundry of his courtiers, declaiming against the philosophers and rationalists, while he pressed all his hearers to study and practise the precepts of Islām. Those courtiers maligned him with the king, calling him an intriguer who had designs on the throne. The king sent and made him an offer of the sovereignty, promising to retire elsewhere himself. Bahā answered that he had no concern with earthly greatness, being a poor recluse; and that he would willingly leave the country, so as to remove from the king's mind all misgivings on his score.

He accordingly quitted Balkh, with a suite of about forty souls, after delivering a public address in the great mosque before the king and people. In this address he foretold the advent of the Moguls to overturn the kingdom, possess the country, destroy Balkh, and drive out the king, who would then flee to the Roman land, and there at length be killed.

So he left Balkh, as the prophet (Muhammed) had fled from Mekka to Medīna. His son Jelālu-'d-Dīn was then five, and the elder brother, 'Alā'u-'d-Dīn, seven years old.

The people everywhere on his road, hearing of his approach or forewarned in dreams of his coming, flocked to meet him and do him honour. Thus he drew near to Bagdād. Here he was met by the great Sheykh Shahābu-'d-Dīn, 'Umer, Suherverdī, the most eminent man of the place, deputed by the Caliph Musta'zim to do him honour. He became the guest of the Sheykh.

The Caliph sent him a present of three thousand sequins, but he declined the gift as being money unlawfully acquired. He also refused to visit the Caliph; but consented to preach in the great mosque after the noon service of worship on the following Friday, the Caliph being present. In his discourse he reproached the Caliph to his face with his evil course of life, and warned him of his approaching slaughter by the Moguls with great cruelty and ignominy. The Caliph again sent him rich presents in money, horses, and valuables, but he refused to accept them.

Before Bahā'u-'d-Dīn quitted Bagdād, intelligence was received there of the siege of Balkh, of its capture, and of its entire destruction, with its twelve thousand mosques, by the Mogul army of five hundred thousand men commanded by Jengīz in person (in A.H. 608, A.D. 1211). Fourteen thousand copies of the Qur'ān were destroyed, fifteen thousand students and professors of the law were slain, and two hundred thousand adult male inhabitants led out and shot to death with arrows.

Bahā'u-'d-Dīn went from Bagdād to Mekka, performed the greater pilgrimage there, proceeding thence to Damascus, and next to Malatia (Melitene, on the Upper Euphrates), where, in A.H. 614 (A.D. 1217), he heard of the death of Jengīz. The Seljūqī Sultan, 'Alā'u-'d-Dīn Keyqubād, was then sovereign of the land of Rome (Rūm, i.e., Asia Minor), and was residing at Sīwās (Sebaste). In A.H. 620 (A.D. 1223) Sultan Jelālu-'d-Dīn, the dispossessed monarch of Kh'ārezm (Chorasmia) was killed in a battle fought by him in Azerbāyjān (Atropatene) against the Sultans of Rome, Syria, and Egypt, when his forces were totally defeated. And thus ended that great dynasty, after ruling about a hundred and forty years.

Bahā'u-'d-Dīn went from Malatia and remained four years near Erzinjān (the ancient Aziris, on the Western Euphrates), in Armenia, at a college built for him by a saintly lady, 'Ismet Khātūn. She was the wife of the local sovereign, Melik Fakhru-'d-Dīn. She and her husband both died, and then Bahā'u-'d-Dīn passed on to Larenda (in Cataonia), in Asia Minor, and remained there about seven years at the head of a college, the princess Melika'i-Jihān, his mother, being still with him.

Here it was that his younger son, Jelālu-'d-Dīn Muhammed, the future author of the Mesnevī, attained to man's estate, being then eighteen years old; when, in A.H. 623 (A.D. 1226), he married a young lady named Gevher Khātūn, daughter of the Lala Sherefu-'d-Dīn, of Samarqand. She gave birth in due course to Jelāl's eldest son, 'Alā'u-'d-Dīn.

The king had now returned to his capital, Qonya (the ancient Iconium). Hearing of Bahā'u-'d-Dīn's great learning and sanctity, the king sent and invited him to the capital, where he installed him in a college, and soon professed himself a disciple. Many miracles are related as having been worked at Qonya by Bahā'u-'d-Dīn, who at length died there on Friday, the 18th of Rebī'u-'l-ākhir, A.H. 628 (February A.D. 1231). The Sultan erected a marble mausoleum over his tomb, on which this date is recorded. Many miracles continued to occur at this sanctuary. The Sultan died also a few years later, in A.H. 634 (A.D. 1236).

(After the death of Bahā'u-'d-Dīn Veled, and the acquisition of still greater fame by his son Jelālu-'d-Dīn, who received the honorific title of Khudāvendgār—Lord—the father was distinguished from the son, among the disciples, by the customary title of Mevlānā Buzurg—the Greater or Elder Master. The traditions collected by Eflākī, relating to this period, vary considerably from one another on minor points of date and order of succession, though the main facts come out sufficiently clear.)

3

Jelāl's son, Sultān Veled, related to Eflākī that his father Jelāl used frequently to say, "I and all my disciples will be under the protection of the Great Master, my father, on the day of resurrection; and under His guidance we shall enter the divine presence; God will pardon all of us for His sake."

4

It is related that when the Great Master departed this life, his son, Jelālu-'d-Dīn, was fourteen years old. (This is apparently a copyist's error for "twenty-four." Jalāl is said to have been born in A.H. 604–A.D. 1207.) He married when seventeen (or eighteen); and often did he say in the presence of the congregation of his friends, "The Great Master will remain with me a few years. I shall be in need of Shemsu-'d-Dīn of Tebrīz (the capital of Azerbāyjān); for every prophet has had an Abū-Bekr, as Jesus had His apostles."

5

Shortly after the death of the Great Master Bahā'u-'d-Dīn Veled, news was received by the Sultan 'Alā'u-'d-Dīn of Qonya of the arrival of Sultan Jelālu-'d-Dīn Kh'ārezm-Shāh on the borders of Asia Minor. The Sultan went and prayed at the tomb of the deceased saint, and then prepared to meet the Kh'ārezmians, who were in the neigh8bourhood of Erzenu-'r-Rūm (Erzen of the Romans, the ancient Arzes, now Erzerum). Scouts brought in the intelligence that the Kh'ārezmians were very numerous; and great anxiety prevailed among the Sultan's troops. He resolved to see for himself.

He put on a disguise and set out with a few followers, on fleet horses, for the Kh'ārezmian camp. They gave out that they were nomad Turks of the neighbourhood, their ancestors having come from the Oxus; that latterly the Sultan had withdrawn his favour from them; and that, in consequence, they had for some time past been looking for the Kh'ārezmian advent. This was reported to the king, Jelālu-'d-Dīn, who sent for them and received them kindly, giving them tents and assigning them rations.

During the night King Jelālu-'d-Dīn began to reflect that every one had hitherto spoken well of Sultan 'Alā'u-'d-Dīn, and a doubt arose in his mind in consequence respecting the story of these newcomers, especially as he learned that the Sultan was on his march to meet him. Consulting with the Prince of Erzenu-'r-Rūm, further perquisition was postponed until the morrow.

But at midnight the deceased saint of Qonya, Bahā-Veled, appeared in a dream to Sultan 'Alā'u-'d-Dīn, and warned him to fly at once. The Sultan awoke, found it was a dream, and went to sleep again. The saint now appeared a second time. The Sultan saw himself seated on his throne, and the saint coming to him, smiting him on the breast with his staff, and angrily saying, "Why sleepest thou? Arise!"

Now the Sultan did arise, quietly called his people, saddled horses, and stole away out of the camp. Towards morning King Jelāl caused guards to be placed round the tents of the strangers to watch them. But afterwards, when orders were given to bring them to the king's presence to be questioned, their tents were found to be empty. Pursuit was attempted, but in vain.

After an interval the two armies came into collision. The Sultan of Qonya was victorious. From that time forward, whenever difficulties threatened, he always betook himself to the shrine of the saint, Bahā Veled, who always answered his prayers.

(As Sultan Jelālu-'d-Dīn Kh'ārezm-Shāh has already been stated to have died in battle in Azerbāyjān in A.D. 1223, whereas the saint of Qonya did not die until A.D. 1231 eight years afterwards, the discrepancy of that date with the present anecdote is irreconcilable.)

6

The Great Master, Bahā Veled, used to say that while he himself lived no other teacher would be his equal, but that when his son, Jelālu-'d-Dīn, should succeed him at his death, that son of his would equal and even surpass him.

7

Seyyid Burhānu-'d-Dīn Termīzī is related to have said that one night the door of the mausoleum of Bahā Veled opened of itself, and that a great glory shone forth from it, which gradually filled his house, so that no shadow fell from anything. The glory then gradually filled the city in like manner, spreading thence over the whole face of nature. On beholding this prodigy the Seyyid swooned away.

This vision is a sure indication that the whole human race will one day own themselves the disciples of the descendants of the great saint.

Before he quitted Balkh, Bahā Veled one day saw a man performing his devotions in the great mosque in his shirt sleeves, with his coat upon his back. Bahā reproved him, telling him to put on his coat properly and decently, then to continue his devotions. "And what if I will not?" asked the man in a disdainful tone. "Thy dead-like soul will obey my command, quit thy body, and thou wilt die!" answered Bahā. Instantly the man fell dead; and crowds flocked to become disciples to the saint who spoke with such power and authority.

9

When Sultan 'Alā'u-'d-Dīn had fortified Qonya, he invited Bahā Veled to mount to the terraced roof of the palace, thence to survey the walls and towers. After his inspection, Bahā remarked to the Sultan, "Against torrents, and against the horsemen of the enemy, thou hast raised a goodly defence. But what protection hast thou built against those unseen arrows, the sighs and moans of the oppressed, which overleap a thousand walls and sweep whole worlds to destruction? Go to, now! strive to acquire the blessings of thy subjects. These are a stronghold, compared to which the walls and turrets of the strongest castles are as nothing."

10

On one occasion Sultan 'Alā'u-'d-Dīn paid a visit to Bahā Veled. In lieu of his hand the latter offered the tip of his staff to be kissed by the Sultan, who thought within himself: "The proud scholar!" Bahā read the Sultan's thoughts as a seer, and remarked in reply thereto: "Mendicant students are bound to be humble and lowly. Not so a

Sultan of the Faith who has attained to the utmost circumference of the orbit thereof, and revolves therein."

11

A certain Sheykh Hajjāj, a disciple of Bahā Veled and one of God's elect not known to the herd of mankind, quitted the college after the decease of his teacher, and betook himself to his former trade of a weaver, therewith to gain an honest livelihood. He used to buy the coarsest brown bread of unsifted flour, mash this up with water, and break his fast with this sop alone. All the rest of his earnings he saved up until they would reach to two or three hundred piastres. This sum he would then carry to the college, and place it in the shoes of his teacher's son, Jelālu-'d-Dīn, the new rector. This practice he continued so long as he lived.

At his death a professional washer was appointed to perform the last ablution for Sheykh Hajjāj. In the execution of his office the washer was about to touch the privities of the deceased, when the defunct seized his hand with so strong a grip as to make him scream with pain and fright. The friends came to rescue him, but they were unable to release the imprisoned hand. They therefore sent word to Jelālu-'d-Dīn of what had occurred. He came and saw, knew the reason, and whispered into the ear of the deceased man: "The poor simpleton has been unaware of the high station of thy sanctity. Pardon his unintentional transgression for my sake." Immediately the poor washer's hand was released; but three days afterwards he was himself washed and borne lifeless to his grave.

12

The Sultan had a governor of his childhood still living, the Emīr Bedru-'d-Dīn Guhertāsh, commonly known as the Dizdār

(Castellan), whom he held in great esteem. One day, as Bahā Veled was lecturing in the mosque, in presence of the Sultan and his court, he suddenly called upon the Dizdār to recite any ten verses of the Qur'ān, saying he would then expound them to the congregation. The Dizdār had been admiring the eloquence of the preacher's expositions. Upon this sudden call, without the slightest hesitation and without ever having committed them to memory, he recited the first ten verses of chapter xxiii., "The believers have attained to prosperity," &c., which Bahā forthwith explained in such a manner as to draw down the plaudits of the assembly. The Dizdār, with the Sultan's permission, went to the foot of the pulpit and declared himself a disciple to Bahā. "Then," said the preacher, "as a thank-offering for this happy event, do thou build and endow a college where my descendants shall teach their disciples after me." The Dizdār did so, and richly endowed it. This is the college where Jelālu-'d-Dīn afterwards lived. When the Dizdār died he left all his possessions to enrich the foundation.

13

The Sultan had a dream (something like one of Nebuchadnezzar's). He saw himself with a head of gold, a breast of silver, a belly of brass, thighs of lead, and shanks of tin. Bahā Veled explained the dream as follows:—"All will go well in the kingdom during thy lifetime. It will be as silver in the days of thy son; as brass in the next generation, when the rabble will get the upper hand. Troubles will thicken during the next reign; and after that the kingdom of Rome will go to ruin, the house of Seljūq will come to an end, and unknown upstarts will seize the reins of government."

CHAPTER II

*Seyyid Burhānu-'d-Dīn, Sirr-Dān, el Muhaqqiq, el Huseynī,
of the posterity of Yā-Sīn (Muhammed).*

(He is called Seyyid, the "Syud" of our East India authorities,
for the reason that he was a descendant of the prophet, of
whom Yā-Sīn is one of the titles, as it is also the name of
the thirty-sixth chapter of the Qur'ān, at the head of which
the two letters stand which form the name. Burhānu-'d-Dīn
means The Proof of the Religion; Sirr-Dān signifies The
Confidant, one who possesses a knowledge of a secret or
secrets, a mystery or mysteries. Muhaqqiq is one who verifies,
who probes the truth; and Huseynī indicates that the Seyyid
was of the branch of Huseyn, the younger of the two sons of
Fātima, Muhammed's only child that left posterity.)

1

Seyyid Burhānu-'d-Dīn was popularly known by the name of
Sirr-Dān at Balkh, Bukhārā and Termīz. His discourse was
continually running upon the subjects of spiritual and mental
phenomena, of the mysteries of earth and of heaven.

When Bahā Veled quitted Balkh, the Seyyid went to Termīz, and there secluded himself as a hermit. After a while again he began to lecture in public on the significations of knowledge. Suddenly, one morning, that of Friday the 18th of Rebī'u-'l-ākhir, A.H. 628 (February,14 1231 A.D.), he cried out most bitterly, in a flood of tears, "Alas! my master has passed away from this tabernacle of dust to the abode of sincerity!" His words and the date were noted down, and, on inquiry, after his arrival in Qonya, were found to correspond exactly with the moment of Bahā Veled's decease.

2

For forty days the disciples at Termīz mourned for the death of the great teacher. At the end of that period the Seyyid said: "The son of my master, his successor, Jelālu-'d-Dīn Muhammed, is left alone and is wishing to see me. I must go to the land of Rome and place myself at his service, delivering over to him the trust which my teacher confided to my safe-keeping."

3

When the Seyyid reached Qonya, Bahā Veled had been dead about a year, and Jelāl had gone to Larenda. The Seyyid applied himself for several months to devotional seclusion in one of the mosques of Qonya; after which he sent off a letter to Jelāl by the hands of two mendicants, saying: "Come and meet this stranger to thee at the resting-place of thy father, for Larenda is not a place of permanency for thee. From that hill (on which Bahā's mausoleum was built) a fire will shower down on the city of Qonya."

After reading this epistle Jelāl returned to Qonya with all possible despatch. There he went at once to visit the Seyyid, who came forth from the mosque to receive him. They embraced. They

now entered into conversation on various subjects. So delighted
was the Seyyid with the expositions set forth by Jelāl that he kissed
the soles of his feet, and exclaimed: "A hundredfold hast thou
surpassed thy father in all knowledge of the humanities; but thy
father was versed also in the mysteries of mute reality and ecstasy.
From this day forward my desire is that thou shouldest also acquire
that knowledge,—the knowledge possessed by the prophets and
the saints, which is entitled The Science of Divine Intuition—the
science spoken of by God: 'We have taught him a science from
within us.' This knowledge did I acquire from my teacher; do thou
receive it from me, so that thou mayest be the heir to thy father in
spiritual matters as well as in things temporal. Thou wilt then be
his second self."

Jelāl complied with all the Seyyid pressed upon him. He took
the Seyyid to his college, and for nine years received instruction
from him. Some accounts make it appear that Jelāl first became the
Seyyid's disciple at this time; but others go to show that Bahā Veled
gave Jelāl as a pupil to the Seyyid at Balkh, and that the Seyyid
used now and then to carry Jelāl about on his shoulders, like as is
practised by the nursing-tutors—lala—of children.

4

Husāmu-'d-Dīn told us that Jelāl had informed him of the
following occurrence:—

The Seyyid once arrived at a certain city in Khurāsān named
Sāmānek. The chief people went forth to meet him and show him
honour, all excepting the Sheykhu-'l-Islām of the place (the local
vice-chancellor). Nevertheless the Seyyid went to pay his respects
to the legal functionary. The latter went barefoot to the door of the
house to meet the Seyyid, whose hand he kissed, and to whom he
offered excuses for his seeming lack of courtesy.

In reply, the Seyyid said to him: "I am come to inform you that, on the 10th day of next month, Ramazān, you will have occasion to go forth to a hot-bath. On your way thither you will be assassinated by the emissaries of the Old Man of the Mountain. This I communicate to thee, that thou mayest set thy affairs in order, and repent thee of thy sins."

The Sheykhu-'l-Islām fell at the Seyyid's feet, wailing; but the latter remarked: "This is of no avail. Events are in God's hands, and He has so ordered it. Still, as thou showest so much contrition, I may add, for thy consolation, that thou wilt die in the faith, and shalt not be cut off from the divine mercy and grace."

And so it happened as thus predicted. The assassins took his life on the very day foretold by the Seyyid.

(The stronghold, Alamūt, of the Old Man of the Mountain, was stormed by forces sent against it by Helagū, grandson of Jengīz, in about the year A.H. 654 (A.D. 1256). The last prince of the dynasty was sent to China, and there put to death by the emperor; and thus these detestable scourges of humanity were at length suppressed.)

5

After a certain time the Seyyid asked permission of Jelāl to go for a while to Qaysariyya (Cæsarea), but Jelāl could not spare him. So he remained at Qonya still.

Somewhat later a party of friends took the Seyyid out for a ride among the vineyards. The thought occurred to him that, without saying anything to anybody, he might now easily abscond and get away to Qaysariyya. Scarcely had he conceived this vagabond idea than his beast reared with him, threw him, and broke his leg. His friends raised him, set him again on his horse, and conducted him to a neighbouring country-house to which Jelāl had also come.

On seeing Jelāl the Seyyid exclaimed to him, "Is this the proper way to reward your teacher—to break his leg?" Jelāl at once ordered the Seyyid's boot to be removed, and saw that his foot and toes were crushed. He now passed his hands along the injured limb and blew on it. The limb was at once restored whole. Jelāl now granted permission, and the Seyyid forthwith proceeded to Qaysariyya.

6

When the time was come that the Seyyid should die, he told his servant to prepare for him an ewer of warm water, and to go. The water was made ready, placed in the Seyyid's room, and the servant went forth. The Seyyid called after him: "Go and proclaim that the stranger Seyyid has departed to the other world." He then bolted the door, that none should enter to him.

The servant, however, had his curiosity excited by those words, and went back to the door, to listen and to see what might happen. Through a chink he saw his master perform an ablution, arrange his dress, lie down on his couch, and cry out: "All ye angels, saints, and heavens, who have at any time intrusted to me a secret, come to me now and receive back your charges. Ye are here all present."

He then recited the following hymn:—

God, my beloved, darling God, adored, to me incline;
My soul receive; intoxicate, release poor me distraught.
In Thee alone my heart finds peace; it fire with love divine;
Take it unto Thyself; to it both worlds are naught.

These were the Seyyid's last words, ere he yielded up his spirit. The servant carried the news to the Seyyid's friends, who gathered together, carried him forth, and buried him.

A mausoleum was raised over his grave by a rich and powerful disciple. The departed saint would not allow a cupola to stand. Twice the dome was shaken down by earthquakes, and in a dream the Seyyid himself forbade its third edification.

After the usual forty days of mourning, a letter was sent to Jelāl, who at once journeyed from Qonya to Qaysariyya, and prayed at the tomb of his deceased teacher, returning home again afterwards.

CHAPTER III

Mevlānā Jelālu-'d-Dīn Muhammed, the Revered
Mystery of God upon Earth.

1

Jelālu-'d-Dīn is related to have been born at Balkh on the 6th
of Rebī'u-'l-evvel, A.H. 604 (29th September 1207).

When five years old, he used at times to become extremely
uneasy and restless, so much so that his attendants used to
take him into the midst of themselves.

The cause of these perturbations was that spiritual forms
and shapes of the absent (invisible world) would arise before
his sight, that is, angelic messengers, righteous genii, and
saintly men—the concealed ones of the bowers of the True
One (spiritual spouses of God), used to appear to him in
bodily shape, exactly as the cherubim and seraphim used to
show themselves to the holy apostle of God, Muhammed,
in the earlier days, before his call to the prophetic office; as
Gabriel appeared to Mary, and as the four angels were seen by
Abraham and Lot; as well as others to other prophets.

His father, Bahā'u-'d-Dīn Veled, the Sultānu-'l-'Ulemā, used on these occasions to coax and soothe him by saying: "These are the Occult Existences. They come to present themselves before you, to offer unto you gifts and presents from the invisible world."

These ecstasies and transports of his began to be publicly known and talked about; and the affectionately honorific title of Khudāvendgār, by which he is so often mentioned, was conferred upon him at this time by his father, who used to address him and speak of him by this title, as "My Lord."

2

His son, Sultan Veled, related that there was a paper in the handwriting of his father, Bahā Veled, which set forth that at Balkh, when Jelāl was six years old, he was taking the air one Friday, on the terraced roof of the house, and reciting the Qur'ān, when some other children of good families came in and joined him there.

After a time, one of these children proposed that they should try and jump from thence on to a neighbouring terrace, and should lay wagers on the result.

Jelāl smiled at this childish proposal, and remarked: "My brethren, to jump from terrace to terrace is an act well adapted for cats, dogs, and the like, to perform; but is it not degrading to man, whose station is so superior? Come now, if you feel disposed, let us spring up to the firmament, and visit the regions of God's realm." As he yet spake, he vanished from their sight.

Frightened at Jelāl's sudden disappearance, the other children raised a shout of dismay, that some one should come to their assistance; when lo, in an instant, there he was again in their midst; but with an altered expression of countenance and blanched cheeks. They all uncovered before him, fell to the earth in humility, and all declared themselves his disciples.

He now told them that, as he was yet speaking to them, a company of visible forms, clad in green raiment, had led him away from them, and had conducted him about the various concentric orbs of the spheres, and through the signs of the Zodiac, showing him the wonders of the world of spirits, and bringing him back to them so soon as their cries had reached his ears.

At that age, he was used not to break his fast more20 often than once in three or four, and sometimes even seven, days.

3

A different witness, a disciple of Jelāl's father, related that Bahā Veled frequently affirmed publicly that his Lord, Jelāl, was of exalted descent, being of the lineage of a king, and also of an hereditary saint.

His maternal grandmother was a daughter of the great Imām Es-Sarakhsī11 (died at Damascus A.H. 571, A.D. 1175), who was of the lineage of the Prophet. The mother of Es-Sarakhsī was descended from the Caliph 'Alī; and Jelāl's paternal grandmother was a daughter of the King of Kh'ārezm, who resided at Balkh.

Jelāl's paternal great-great-grandmother, also, the mother of Ahmed, El-Khatībī, grandfather of Jelāl's father, was a daughter of a king of Balkh. These particulars establish that Jelāl was well descended on both sides, in a mundane and in a spiritual sense. The well-known proverb—

> *Hereditary disposition ever insinuates itself,*
> *proved fully true in his most illustrious case.*

4

When Jelāl was seven years old, he used every morning to recite the very short chapter, cviii., of the Qur'ān—

"Verily we have given unto thee the abounding good. Therefore, do thou perform thy devotions unto thy Lord, and slaughter victims. Verily, he who evil entreateth thee is one who shall leave no issue after him."

He used to weep as he recited these inspired words.

Suddenly, God one day vouchsafed to appear to him visibly. On this he fainted away. Regaining consciousness, he heard a voice from heaven, that said—

O Jelālu-'d-Dīn! By the majesty (jelāl) of Our glory, do thou
henceforward cease to combat with thyself; for We have exalted thee
to the station of ocular vision.

Jelāl vowed, therefore, out of gratitude for this mark of grace, to serve the Lord to the end of his days, to the utmost of his power; in the firm hope that they who followed him would also attain to that high grade of favour and excellence.

5

Two years after the death of his father, Jelāl went from Qonya to Haleb (Aleppo) to study.

As he was known to be a son of Bahā'u-'d-Dīn Veled, and was also an apt scholar, his professor showed him every attention.

Others were offended, and evinced their jealousy at the preference thus accorded to him. They complained to the governor of the city that Jelāl was immoral, as he was in the habit, each night, of quitting his cell at midnight for some unknown purpose. The governor resolved to see and judge for himself. He therefore hid himself in the porter's room.

At midnight, Jelāl came forth from his room, and went straight to the locked gate of the college, watched by the governor. The gate flew open; and Jelāl, followed at a distance by the governor, went through the streets to the locked city gate. This, too, opened of itself; and again both passed forth.

They went on and came to the tomb of Abraham (at Hebron, about 350 miles distant), the "Friend of the All-Merciful." There a domed edifice was seen, filled with a large company of forms in green raiment, who came forth to meet Jelāl, and conducted him into the building.

The governor hereupon lost his senses through fright, and did not recover until after the sun had risen.

Now, he could see nothing of a domed edifice, nor one single human being. He wandered about on a trackless plain for three days and three nights, hungry, thirsty, and footsore. At length he sank under his sufferings.

Meanwhile, the porter of the college had given intelligence of the governor's pursuit after Jelāl. When his officers found that he did not return, they sent a numerous party of guards to seek him. These, on the second day, met Jelāl. He told them where they would find their master. The next day, late, they came up with him, found him to be nearly dead, and brought him home.

The governor became a sincere convert, and a disciple to Jelāl for ever after.

(A parallel tale is told of Jelāl's fetching water from the Tigris for his father by night when he was a little child at Bagdad. There, too, all the gates opened to him of themselves.)

6

It is related that the Seyyid Burhānu-'d-Dīn was often heard to narrate that, when Jelāl was a child, the Seyyid was his governor and tutor. He had often taken Jelāl up on his shoulder, and so carried him to the empyrean. "But now," he would add, "Jelāl has attained to such eminence of station that he carries me up." These sayings of the Seyyid were repeated to Jelāl, who confirmed them with the remark: "It is quite true; and a hundredfold more also; the services rendered to me by that man are infinite."

7

When Jelāl went to Damascus to study, he passed by Sīs in Upper Cilicia. There, in a cave, dwelt forty Christian monks, who had a great reputation for sanctity, but in reality were mere jugglers.

On the approach of Jelāl's caravan to the cave, the monks caused a little boy to ascend into the air, and there remain standing between heaven and earth.

Jelāl noticed this exhibition, and fell into a reverie. Hereupon, the child began to weep and wail, saying that the man in the reverie was frightening him. The monks told him not to be afraid, but to come down. "Oh!" cried the child, "I am as though nailed here, unable to move hand or foot."

The monks became alarmed. They flocked around Jelāl, and begged him to release the child. After a time, he seemed to hear and understand them. His answer was: "Only through the acceptance of Islām by yourselves, all of you, as well as by the child, can he be saved."

In the end they all embraced Islām, and wished to follow Jelāl as his disciples. He recommended them, however, to remain in their cave, as before, to cease from practising jugglery, and to serve God in the spirit and in truth. So he proceeded on his journey.

8

Jelāl remained seven years, or four years, at Damascus; and there he first saw his great friend Shemsu-'d-Dīn of Tebrīz, clothed in his noted black felt and peculiar cap. Shems addressed him; but he turned away, and mixed in the crowd. Soon afterwards, he returned to Qonya by way of Qaysariyya. At this latter place, under the guiding supervision of his spiritual teacher, the Seyyid Burhānu-'d-Dīn, Jelāl fasted three consecutive periods of forty days each, with only a pot of water and two or three loaves of barley bread. He showed no signs of suffering. Burhān now pronounced him perfect in all science, patent and occult, human and spiritual. (Compare chap. ii. No. 3.)

9

In the year A.H. 642 (A.D. 1244), Shemsu-'d-Dīn of Tebrīz came to Qonya.

This great man, after acquiring a reputation of superior sanctity at Tebrīz, as the disciple of a certain holy man, a basket-maker by trade, had travelled about much in various lands, in search of the best spiritual teachers, thus gaining the nickname of Perenda

He prayed to God that it might be revealed to him who was the most occult of the favourites of the divine will, so that he might go to him and learn still more of the mysteries of divine love.

The son of Bahā'u-'d-Dīn Veled, of Balkh, was designated to him as the man most in favour with God. Shems went, accordingly, to Qonya; arriving there on Saturday, the 26th of Jemādà-'l-ākhir, A.H. 642 (December A.D. 1244). He engaged a lodging at an inn, and pretended to be a great merchant. In his room, however, there was nothing but a broken water-pot, an old mat, and a bolster of unbaked clay. He broke his fast once in every ten or twelve days, with a damper soaked in broth of sheep's trotters.

One day, as he was seated at the gate of the inn, Jelāl came by, riding on a mule, in the midst of a crowd of students and disciples on foot.

Shemsu-'d-Dīn arose, advanced, and took hold of the mule's bridle, addressing Jelāl in these words: "Exchanger of the current coins of recondite significations, who knowest the names of the Lord! Tell me: Was Muhammed the greater servant of God, or Bāyezīd of Bestām?"

Jelāl answered him: "Muhammed was incomparably the greater—the greatest of all prophets and all saints."

"Then," rejoined Shemsu-'d-Dīn, "how is it that Muhammed said: 'We have not known Thee, O God, as Thou rightly shouldest be known,' whereas Bāyezīd said: 'Glory unto me! How very great is my glory'?"

On hearing this question, Jelāl fainted away. On recovering his consciousness, he took his new acquaintance home with him. They were closeted together for weeks or months in holy communications.

Jelāl's disciples at length became impatient, raising a fearful and threatening tumult; so that, on Thursday, the 21st of Shewwāl, A.H. 643 (March A.D. 1246), Shemsu-'d-Dīn mysteriously disappeared; and Jelāl adopted, as a sign of mourning for his loss, the drab hat and wide cloak since worn by the dervishes of his order.

It was about this time, also, that he first instituted the musical services observed by that order, as they perform their peculiar waltzing. All men took to music and dancing in consequence. Fanatics objected, out of envy. They said Jelāl was gone mad, even as the chiefs of Mekka had said of old of the Prophet. His supposed malady was attributed to the malefic influence of Shemsu-'d-Dīn of Tebrīz.

10

The widow of Jelāl, Kirā (or Girā) Khātūn, a model of virtue, the Mary of her age, is related to have seen, through a chink in the door of the room where he and Shems were closeted in spiritual communion, that the wall suddenly opened, and six men of majestic mien entered by the cleft.

These strangers, who were of the occult saints, saluted, bowed, and laid a nosegay at the feet of Jelāl, although it was then in the depth of the midwinter season. They remained until near the hour of dawn worship, when they motioned to Shemsu-'d-Dīn to act as leader on the occasion of the service. He excused himself, and Jelāl performed the office. The service of worship over, the six strangers took leave, and passed out by the same cleft in the wall.

Jelāl now came forth from the chamber, bringing the nosegay in his hand. Seeing his wife in the passage, he gave her the nosegay, saying that the strangers had brought it as an offering to her.

The next day, she sent her servant, with a few leaves from her nosegay, to the perfumers' mart of the city, to inquire what might be the flowers composing it, as she had never seen their like before. The merchants were all equally astonished; no one had ever seen such leaves. At length, however, a spice merchant from India, who was then sojourning in Qonya, saw those leaves, and knew them to be the petals of a flower that grows in the south of India, in the neighbourhood of Ceylon.

The wonder now was: How did these Indian flowers get to Qonya; and in the depth of winter, too?

The servant carried the leaves back, and reported to his lady what he had learnt. This increased her astonishment a hundredfold. Just then Jelāl made his appearance, and enjoined on her to take the greatest care of the nosegay, as it had been sent to her by the florists of the lost earthly paradise, through those Indian saints, as a special offering.

It is related that she preserved them as long as she lived, merely giving a few leaves, with Jelāl's express permission, to the Georgian wife of the king. If any one suffered with any disease of the eyes, one leaf from that nosegay, applied to the ailing part, was an instant cure. The flowers never lost their fragrance or freshness. What is musk compared with such?

11

To prove that man lives through God's will alone, and not by blood, Jelāl one day, in the presence of a crowd of physicians and philosophers, had the veins of both his arms opened, and allowed them to bleed until they ceased to flow. He then ordered incisions to be made in various parts of his body; but not one drop of moisture was anywhere obtainable. He now went to a hot bath, washed, performed an ablution, and then commenced the exercise of the sacred dance.

12

One of Jelāl's disciples died, and there was a consultation among his friends as to whether he should be buried in a coffin or without one.

Another disciple, after Jelāl had been consulted, and had told them to do as they pleased, made the observation that it would be better to bury their relative without a coffin. On being asked why, he answered: "A mother can better nurse her child, than can her child's brother. The earth is the mother of the human race, and the wood of a coffin is also the earth's child; therefore, the coffin is the man's brother. Man's corpse should be committed, then, not to a coffin, but to mother earth, his loving, affectionate parent."

Jelāl expressed his admiration for this apposite and sublime doctrine, which, he said, was not to be found written in any then extant book.

The name of the disciple who made this beautiful remark was Kerīmu-'d-Dīn, son of Begh-Tīmūr.

13

Many of the chief disciples of Jelāl have related that he himself explained to them, as his reasons for instituting the musical service of his order, with their dancing, the following reflections:—

God has a great regard for the Roman people. In answer to a prayer of the first Caliph, Abū-Bekr, God made the Romans a chief receptacle of His mercy; and the land of the Romans (Asia Minor) is the most beautiful on the face of the earth. But the people of the land were utterly void of all idea of the riches of a love towards God, and of the remotest shade of a taste for the delights of the inner, spiritual life. The great Causer of all causes caused a source of affection to arise, and out of the wilderness of causelessness raised a means by which I was attracted away from the land of Khurāsān to the country of the Romans. That country He made a home for my children and posterity, in order that, with the elixir of His grace, the copper of their existences might be transmuted into gold and into philosopher-stone, they themselves being received into the communion of saints. When I perceived that they had no inclination for the practice of religious austerities, and no knowledge of the divine mysteries, I imagined to arrange metrical exhortations and musical services, as being captivating for men's minds, and more especially so for the Romans, who are naturally of a lively disposition, and fond of incisive expositions. Even as a sick child is coaxed into taking a salutary, though nauseous medicine, so, in like manner, were the Romans led by art to acquire a taste for spiritual truth.

14

As an instance of the great value attached to the poetry of Jelāl, the following anecdote is related:—

Shemsu-'d-Dīn Hindī, (Prince of Shīrāz in the province of Fars, Southern Persia), wrote a flattering letter to the renowned poet, Sheykh Sa'dī, of Shīrāz (who lived A.H. 571-691, A.D. 1175-1291, and was consequently a contemporary of Jelāl's), begging him to select the best ode, with the most sublime thoughts, that he knew of as existing in Persian, and to send it to him, for presentation to the great Khān of the Moguls (who then ruled over nearly all Asia).

It so happened that the ode by Jelāl had just become known at Shīrāz, which commences:—

"Divine love's voice each instant left and right is heard to sound,
We're bound for heaven. To witness our departure who'll be found?"

This ode had captivated the minds of all the men of culture in the city; and this ode Sa'dī selected, wrote it out, and sent it to the prince, with the remark: "A monarch, of auspicious advent, has sprung up in the land of Rome, from whose privacy these are some of the breathings. Never have more beautiful words been uttered, and never will be. Would that I could go to Rome, and rub my face in the dust under his feet!"

The prince thanked Sa'dī exceedingly, and sent him valuable presents in return. Eventually, Sa'dī did go to "Rome," arrived in Qonya, and had the gratification to kiss the hand of Jelāl. He was well received in that city by the dervish circle.

The prince was himself a disciple of Sheykh . . . 'd-Dīn, of Bakharz (in Khurāsān, about midway between Tūrshīz and Herāt), to whom he sent a copy of the ode, to learn what the Sheykh would think of it. All the learned men of Bakharz assembled round the Sheykh. He read the ode attentively, and then burst out into exclamations of the wildest delight and most fervid admiration, rending his garments, and acting as though mad. At length he calmed down and said: "O wonderful man! O thou champion of the Faith! Thou pole of the heavens and of the earth! Verily, thou art a wonderful Sultan, who hast appeared on earth! In good sooth,

154

all the Sheykhs of bygone ages who were seers, have been frustrated in not having seen this man! They would have supplicated the Lord of Truth to allow them to meet him! But it was not to be; and this mercy will last until the end of time, as has been sung:—

"A fortune, by the men of ancient times in dreams long sought,
Has been vouchsafed to modern men; without their efforts caught."

"One ought to put on ironed shoes, and take in hand an ironed staff, to set out at once and visit this great light. I make it a legacy to all my friends to do so without the least delay, if they have the means and the strength, so as to achieve the happiness and secure the honour of making the acquaintance of this prince, so obtaining the grace and favour of hearing him. His father, Bahā Veled, and his ancestors, were great Sheykhs and most illustrious; their great progenitor having been the first Caliph, Abū-Bekr, the glorious Confirmer of the truth spoken by the Apostle of God. I am myself old and infirm, unequal to the fatigues of travel. Otherwise, I would have walked, not on the soles of my feet, but on the tips of my great toes, to visit that eminent man."

The Sheykh's eldest son, Muzahhiru-'d-Dīn, was there present. To him the Sheykh addressed himself, saying: "My son, I do hope that thy eyes will behold this sacred visage; and, if God so will, convey to him my salutation and my respects."

After the death of the old man, his son went to Rome, had the felicity to see Jelāl, and presented his father's message. He returned to Bakharz; but it is said that a son of his lies buried at Qonya.

15

Kirā Khātūn, the widow of Jelāl, is reported to have related to a friend that there was in their household a candlestick of the height of a man, before which Jelāl used to stand on foot the night through, until daydawn, studying the writings of his father.

One night, a company of the genii, dwellers in the college where Jelāl and his wife lived, appeared to her in a body, to complain of the great inconvenience and suffering to which they were subjected by this practice of Jelāl's, and saying: "We can put up with it no longer. Take care, lest we do a mischief to some one in the college."

The lady reported this complaint of the genii to her husband. He merely smiled, and took no further notice of the matter for several days.

At the end of that time, however, he spoke of it, and told his wife to trouble herself no more about the threat of the genii, as he had converted them all. They had become disciples of his, and would certainly do no harm to any friend or dependent of their teacher.

16

It was related by one of the chief of Jelāl's disciples, a butcher by trade, a trainer of dogs for the chase, and a purveyor of horses of the best kind, which he used to sell to princes and grandees at high prices, that, at a certain time, Jelāl was much exercised by visions from the spiritual world, so that for forty days he was as though beside himself, passing through the streets with his head bare, and his turban twisted round his neck.

After that, he came suddenly one day, bathed in perspiration, to the butcher, and said he wanted a certain unbroken horse to be saddled for him immediately. The butcher, with the help of three stable-men, managed with the utmost difficulty to saddle the horse and bring him out. Jelāl mounted him without opposition, and set off in a southerly direction. The butcher asked whether he should accompany him, and Jelāl replied: "Give me your prayers and holy good wishes."

In the evening Jelāl returned covered with dust. The poor horse, though of gigantic frame, was reduced to mere skin and bone, being nearly broken-backed with fatigue.

The next day he came again, and asked for another horse, better than the one of yesterday, mounted it, and rode off. He returned at the hour of sunset devotions, and this horse also was reduced to a pitiable condition. The butcher dared not offer a word of remonstrance.

On the third day he came again, mounted a third horse, and returned as before, at sunset. He sat down now in the most composed manner possible, and called out cheerily: "Good news! Glad tidings, O ye of the Faith! That dog of hell has gone back to his pit of fire!"

The butcher was too much astonished at his manner to feel any inclination to inquire what these words might mean; but a certain number of days afterwards, a large caravan came into Qonya from Syria, and brought news that the Mogul army had besieged Damascus, and had reduced it to straits.

Helaw Khan (Holagu, Helagu) had taken Bagdad in A.H. 655 (A.D. 1257-58). Two years later, A.H. 657 (A.D. 1259-60), he advanced against Aleppo and Syria, sending his general, Ketbuga, against Damascus with a numerous army. He laid siege to the city. But the inhabitants witnessed, with their very own eyes, that Jelāl came and joined himself there to the forces of Islām. He inflicted defeat on the Mogul forces, who were compelled to retreat, totally frustrated.

The butcher was overjoyed at this welcome intelligence, and went forthwith to communicate the news to Jelāl. The latter smilingly replied: "Yes, yes! Jelālu-'d-Dīn was the horseman who obtained a victory over the enemy, and showed himself a Sultan in the eyes of the people of Islām." On hearing this, his disciples rent the air with their shouts of joy and triumph, and the townspeople of Qonya decked out and illuminated the city, holding public rejoicings.

This miracle of power became noised abroad, and everywhere Jelāl's friends and adherents were transported with ecstasy at its occurrence.

17

On one occasion a rich merchant of Tebrīz came to Qonya. He inquired of his agents there who was the most eminent man of learning and piety in the city, as he wished to go and pay his respects to him. He remarked to them: "It is not merely for the sake of making money that I travel about in every country on earth; I desire also to make the acquaintance of every man of eminence I can find in each city."

His correspondents told him that the Sheykhu-'l-Islām of the capital had a great reputation for learning and piety, and that they would be proud to present him to that celebrated luminary. Accordingly, he selected a number of rarities from among his store, to the value of thirty sequins; and the party set out to visit the great lawyer.

The merchant found the dignitary lodged in a great palace, with guards at the gate, crowds of servants and attendants in the courtyard, and eunuchs, pages, grooms, ushers, chamberlains, and the like, in the halls.

Turning to his conductors, he expressed some doubt as to whether they had not, by mistake, brought him to the king's palace. They quieted his fears, and led him into the presence of the great fountain of legal erudition. He felt a very great dislike for all he saw; and he remarked to his friends: "A great lawyer is never anything the worse for possessing a clear conscience. A physician may himself indulge in sweetmeats; but he does not prescribe them to a patient suffering with fever."

He now offered his presents; and then inquired of the great lawyer whether he could solve a doubt under which he was then labouring. This he stated as follows:—"Of late, I have been sustaining a series of losses. Can you indicate a way by which I may escape from that unfortunate position? I give, every year, the fortieth part of my liable possessions to the poor; and I distribute alms besides, to the extent of my power. I cannot conceive, therefore, why I am unfortunate."

Other remarks he made also to the same effect. They appeared to be lost on the great luminary, who affected to be otherwise preoccupied. At length the merchant took leave without obtaining a solution to his difficulty.

The day following he inquired of his friends whether there did not chance to be, in the great city, some poor mendicant of exemplary piety, to whom he might offer his respects, and from whom he might, haply, learn what he longed to know, together with advice that would be of service to him. They answered: "Just such a man as thou describest is our Lord, Jelālu-'d-Dīn. He has forsaken all pleasures, save only his love towards God. Not only has he given up all concern for worldly matters, he has also renounced all care as to a future state. He passes his nights, as well as his days, in the worship of God; and he is a very ocean of knowledge in all temporal and spiritual subjects."

The Tebrīz merchant was enchanted with this information. He begged to see that holy man, the bare mention of whose virtues had filled him with delight. They accordingly conducted him to the college of Jelāl, the merchant having privately furnished himself with a rouleau of fifty sequins in gold as his offering to the saint.

When they reached the college, Jelāl was sitting alone in the lecture-hall, immersed in the study of some books. The party made their obeisances, and the merchant felt himself completely overpowered at the aspect of the venerable teacher; so that he burst into tears, and could not utter a word. Jelāl addressed him, therefore, as follows:—

"The fifty sequins thou hast provided as thy offering are accepted. But better for thee than these are the two hundred sequins thou hast lost. God, whose glory be exalted, had determined to visit thee with a sore judgment and a heavy trial; but, through this thy visit here, He hath pardoned thee, and the trial is averted from thee. Be not dismayed. From this day forth thou shalt not suffer loss; and that which thou hast already suffered shall be made up to thee."

The merchant was equally astonished and delighted at these words; more so, however, when Jelāl proceeded with his discourse: "The cause and reason of thy bygone losses and misfortunes was, that, on a certain day thou wast in the west of Firengistān (Europe), where thou wentest into a certain ward of a certain city, and there sawest a poor Firengī (European) man, one of the greatest of God's cherished saints, who was lying stretched out at the corner of a market-place. As thou didst pass by him, thou spattest on him, evincing aversion from him. His heart was grieved by thy act and demeanour. Hence the visitations that have afflicted thee. Go thou, then, and make thy peace with him, asking his forgiveness, and offering him our salutations."

The merchant was petrified at this announcement. Jelāl then asked him: "Wilt thou that we this instant show him to thee?" So saying, he placed his hand on the wall of the apartment, and told the merchant to behold. Instantly, a doorway opened in the wall, and the merchant thence perceived that man in Firengistān, lying down in a market-place. At this sight he bowed down his head and rent his garments, coming away from the saintly presence in a state of stupor. He remembered all these incidents as facts.

Immediately commencing his preparations, he set out without delay, and reached the city in question. He inquired for the ward he wished to visit, and for the man whom he had offended. Him he discovered lying down, stretched out as Jelāl had shown him. The merchant dismounted from his beast, and made his obeisance to the prostrate Firengī dervish, who at once addressed him thus: "What wilt thou that I do? Our Lord Jelāl suffereth me not; or otherwise, I had a desire to make thee see the power of God, and what I am. But now, draw near."

The Firengī dervish then clasped the merchant to his bosom, kissed him repeatedly on both cheeks, and then added: "Look now, that thou mayest see my Lord and Teacher, my spiritual Master, and that thou mayest witness a marvel." The merchant looked. He saw the Lord Jelāl immersed in a holy dance, chanting this hymn, and entranced with sacred music:—

"His kingdom's vast and pure; each sort its fitting place finds there;
Cornelian, ruby, clod, or pebble be thou on His hill.
Believe, He seeks thee; disbelieve, He'll haply cleanse thee fair;
Be here a faithful Abū-Bekr; Firengī there; at will."

When the merchant happily reached Qonya on his return, he gave the salutations of the Firengī saint, and his respects, to Jelāl; and distributed much substance among the disciples. He settled at Qonya, and became a member of the fraternity of the Pure Lovers of God.

18

Jelāl was one day passing by a street, where two men were quarrelling. He stood on one side. One of the men called out to the other: "Say what thou will; thou shalt hear from me a thousandfold for every word thou mayest utter."

Hereupon Jelāl stepped forward and addressed this speaker, saying: "No, no! Whatsoever thou have to say, say it to me; and for every thousand thou mayest say to me, thou shalt hear from me one word."

On hearing this rebuke, the adversaries were abashed, and made their peace with one another.

19

One day, a very learned professor brought all his pupils to pay their respects to Jelāl.

On their way to him, the young men agreed together to put some questions to Jelāl on certain points of Arabic grammar, with the design of comparing his knowledge in that science with that of their professor, whom they looked upon as unequalled.

When they were seated, Jelāl addressed them on various fitting subjects for a while, and thereby paved the way for the following anecdote:—

"An ingenuous jurist was once travelling with an Arabic grammarian, and they chanced to come to a ruinous well.

"The jurist hereupon began to recite the text 'And of a ruined well.'

"The Arabic word for 'well' he pronounced 'bīr,' with the vowel long. To this the grammarian instantly objected, telling the jurist to pronounce that word with a short vowel and hiatus—bi'r, so as to be in accord with the requirements of classical purity.

"A dispute now arose between the two on the point. It lasted all the rest of the day, and well on into a pitchy dark night; every author being ransacked by them, page by page, each sustaining his own theory of the word. No conclusion was arrived at, and each disputant remained of his own opinion still.

"It so happened in the dark, that the grammarian slipped37 into the well, and fell to the bottom. There he set up a wail of entreaty: 'O my most courteous fellow-traveller, lend thy help to extricate me from this most darksome pit.'

"The jurist at once expressed his most pleasurable willingness to lend him that help, with only one trifling condition—that he should confess himself in error, and consent to suppress the hiatus in the word 'bi'r.' The grammarian's answer was 'Never.' So in the well he remained."

"Now," said Jelāl, "to apply this to yourselves. Unless you will consent to cast out from your hearts the 'hiatus' of indecision and of self-love, you can never hope to escape from the noisome pit of self-worship,—the well of man's nature and of fleshly lusts. The dungeon of 'Joseph's well' in the human breast is this very 'self-worship;' and from it you will not escape, nor will you ever attain to those heavenly regions—'the spacious land of God'"

On hearing these pregnant words, the whole assembly of undergraduates uncovered their heads, and with fervent zeal professed themselves his spiritual disciples.

20

There was a great and good governor (apparently) of Qonya, of the name of Mu'īnu-'d-Dīn, whose title was the Perwāna (moth or fly-wheel, viz., of the far-distant Mogul Emperor, resident at the court of the king). He was a great friend to the dervishes, to the learned, and to Jelāl, whose loving disciple he was.

One day, a company of the dervishes and learned men united in extolling the Perwāna to the skies, in Jelāl's presence. He assented to all they advanced in that respect, and added: "The Perwāna merits a hundredfold all your eulogiums. But there is another side to the question, which may be exemplified by the following anecdote:—

"A company of pilgrims were once proceeding towards38 Mekka, when the camel of one of the party fell down in the desert, totally exhausted. The camel could not be got to rise again. Its load was, therefore, transferred to another beast, the fallen brute was abandoned to its fate, and the caravan resumed its journey.

"Ere long the fallen camel was surrounded by a circle of ravenous wild beasts,—wolves, jackals, &c. But none of these ventured to attack him. The members of the caravan became aware of this singularity, and one of them went back to investigate the

163

matter. He found that an amulet had been left suspended on the animal's neck; and this he removed. When he had retreated to a short distance, the hungry brutes fell upon the poor camel, and soon tore him piecemeal."

"Now," said Jelāl, "this world is in an exactly similar category with that poor camel. The learned of the world are the company of pilgrims, and our (Jelāl's) existence among them is the amulet suspended round the neck of the camel—the world. So long as we remain so suspended, the world will go on, the caravan will proceed. But so soon as the divine mandate shall be spoken: 'O thou submissive spirit, come thou back to thy Lord, content and approved' and we be removed from the neck of the world-camel, people will see how it shall fare with the world,—how its inhabitants shall be driven,—what shall become of its sultans, its doctors, its scribes."

It is said that these words were spoken a short time before Jelāl's death. When he departed this life, not much time elapsed ere the Sultan, with many of his great men of learning and nobles, followed him to the grave, while troubles of all kinds overwhelmed the land for a season, until God again vouchsafed it peace.

21

During one of his expositions, Jelāl said: "Thou seest naught, save that thou seest God therein."

A dervish came forward and raised the objection that the term "therein" indicated a receptacle, whereas it could not be predicated of God that He is comprehensible by any receptacle, as this would imply a contradiction in terms. Jelāl answered him as follows:—

"Had not that unimpeachable proposition been true, we had not proffered it. There is therein, forsooth, a contradiction in terms; but it is a contradiction in time, so that the receptacle and the recepted may differ,—may be two distinct things; even as the universe of God's qualities is the receptacle of the universe of God's essence. But, these two universes are really one. The first of them is not He; the second of them is not other than He. Those, apparently, two things are in truth one and the same. How, then, is a contradiction in terms implied? God comprises the exterior and the interior. If we cannot say He is the interior, He will not include the interior. But He comprises all, and in Him all things have their being. He is, then, the receptacle also, comprising all existences, as the says: 'He comprises all things.'"

The dervish was convinced, bowed, and declared himself a disciple.

22

Jelāl was one day seated in the shop of his great disciple the Goldbeater, Salāhu-'d-Dīn; and was surrounded by a circle of other disciples, listening to his discourse; when an old man came rushing in, beating his breast, and uttering loud lamentations. He entreated Jelāl to help him in his endeavours to recover his little son, a child seven years old, lost for several days past, in spite of every effort made to find him.

Jelāl expressed his disapprobation at the extreme importance the old man appeared to attach to his loss; and said: "Mankind in general have lost their God. Still, one does not hear that they go about in quest of Him, beating their breasts and making a great noise. What, then, has happened to thee so very particular, that thou makest all this fuss, and degradest thyself, an elder, by these symptoms of grief for the loss of a little child? Why seekest thou not for a time the Lord of the whole world, begging assistance of Him, that peradventure thy lost Joseph may be found, and thou be comforted, as was Jacob on the recovery of his child?"

The old man at once followed Jelāl's advice, and begged forgiveness of God. Just then, news was brought him there that his son had been found. Many who were witnesses of these circumstances became devoted followers of Jelāl.

23

Jelāl was one day lecturing, when a young man of distinction came in, pushed his way, and took a seat higher up than an old man, one of the audience.

Jelāl at once remarked: "In days of yore it was the command of God, that, if any young man should take precedence of an elder, the earth should at once swallow him up; such being the divine punishment for that offence. Now, however, I see that young men, barely out of leading-strings, show no respect for age, but trample over those in years. They have no dread of the earth's swallowing them up, nor any fear of being transformed into apes. It happened, however, that one morning the Victorious Lion of God, 'Alī, son of Abū-Tālib, was hasting from his house to perform his devotions at dawn in the mosque of the Prophet. On his way, he overtook an old man, a Jew, who was going in the same direction. The future Caliph, out of innate nobility and politeness of nature, had respect for the Jew's age, and would not pass him, though the Jew's pace was slow. When 'Alī reached the mosque, the Prophet was already bowed down in his devotions, and was about to chant the 'Gloria;' but, by God's command, Gabriel came down, laid his hand on the Prophet's shoulder, and stopped him, lest 'Alī should lose the merit attaching to his being present at the opening of the dawn service; for it is more meritorious to perform that early service once, than to fulfil the devotions of a hundred years at other hours of the day. The Prophet has said: 'The first act of reverence at dawn worship is of more value than the world and all that is therein.'

166

"When the Apostle of God had concluded his worship, offered up his customary prayers, and recited his usual lessons from the Qur'ān, he turned, and asked of Gabriel the occult cause of his interruption at that time. Gabriel replied that God had not seen fit that 'Alī should be deprived of the merit attaching to the performance of the first portion of the dawn worship, through the respect he had shown to the old Jew he had overtaken, but whom he would not pass.

"Now," remarked Jelāl, "when a saint like 'Alī showed so much respect for a poor old misbelieving Jew, and when God viewed his respectful consideration in so highly favourable a manner, you may all infer how He will view any honour and veneration shown to an elderly saint of approved piety, whose beard has grown grey in the service of God, and whose companions are the elect of their Maker, whose chosen servant he is; and what reward He will mete out in consequence. For, in truth, glory and power belong to God, to the Apostle, and to the believers, as God hath Himself declared 'Unto God belongeth the power, and to the apostle, and to the believers.'

"If then," added he, "ye wish to be prosperous in your affairs, take fast hold on the skirts of your spiritual elders. For, without the blessing of his pious elders, a young man will never live to be old, and will never attain the station of a spiritual elder."

24

One day Jelāl took as his text the following words—"Verily, the most discordant of all sounds is the voice of the asses." He then put the question: "Do my friends know what this signifies?"

The congregation all bowed, and entreated him to expound it to them. Jelāl therefore proceeded:—

"All other brutes have a cry, a lesson, and a doxology, with which they commemorate their Maker and Provider. Such are, the yearning cry of the camel, the roar of the lion, the bleat of the gazelle, the buzz of the fly, the hum of the bee, &c.

"The angels in heaven, and the genii, have their doxologies also, even as man has his doxology—his Magnificat, and various forms of worship for his heart (or mind) and for his body.

"The poor ass, however, has nothing but his bray. He sounds this bray on two occasions only: when he desires his female, and when he feels hunger. He is the slave of his lust and of his gullet.

"In like manner, if man have not in his heart a doxology for God, a cry, and a love, together with a secret and a care in his mind, he is less than an ass in God's esteem; for He has said 'They are like the camels; nay, they are yet more erring.'" He then related the following anecdote:—

"In bygone days there was a monarch, who, by way of trial, requested another sovereign to send him three things, the worst of their several kinds that he could procure; namely, the worst article of food, the worst dispositioned thing, and the worst animal.

"The sovereign so applied to sent him some cheese, as the worst food; an Armenian slave, as the worst-dispositioned thing; and an ass, as the worst of animals. In the superscription to the epistle sent with these offerings, the sovereign quoted the verse of Scripture pointed out above."

25

On a certain day, the Lord Jelālu-'d-Dīn went forth to the country residence of the saint Husāmu-'d-Dīn, riding on an ass. He remarked: "This is the saddle-beast of the righteous. Several of the prophets have ridden on asses: as Seth, Ezra, Jesus, and Muhammed."

It so chanced that one of his disciples was also mounted on an ass. The creature suddenly began to bray; and the rider, annoyed at the occurrence, struck the ass on the head several times.

Jelāl remonstrated: "Why strike the poor brute? Strikest thou him because he bears thy burden? Returnest thou not thanks for that thou art the rider, and he the vehicle? Suppose now, which God forbid, that the reverse were the case. What wouldst thou have done? His cry arises from one or the other of two causes, his gullet or his lust. In this respect, he shares the common lot of all creatures. They are all continually thus actuated. All, then, would have to be scolded and beaten over the head."

The disciple was abashed. He dismounted, kissed the hoof of his ass, and caressed him.

26

On a certain occasion, one of his disciples complained to Jelāl of the scantiness of his means and the extent of his needs. Jelāl answered: "Out upon thee! Get thee gone! Henceforward, count me not a friend of thine; and so, peradventure, wealth may come to thee." He then related the following anecdote:—

"It happened, once, that a certain disciple of the Prophet said to him: 'I love thee!' The Prophet answered: 'Why tarriest thou, then? Haste to put on a breastplate of steel, and set thy face to encounter misfortunes. Prepare thyself, also, to endure straitness, the special gift of the friends and lovers (of God and His Apostle)!'"

Another anecdote, also, he thus narrated: "A Gnostic adept once asked of a rich man which he loved best, riches or sin. The latter answered that he loved riches best. The other replied: 'Thou sayest not the truth. Thou better lovest sin and calamity. Seest thou not that thou leavest thy riches behind, whilst thou carriest thy sin and thy calamity about with thee, making thyself reprehensible in the sight of God! Be a man! Exert thyself to carry thy riches with thee, and sin not; since thou lovest thy riches. What thou hast to do is this: Send thy riches to God ere thou goest before Him thyself; peradventure, they may work thee some advantage; even as God hath said 'And that which ye send before, for your souls, of good works, shall ye find with God. He is the best and the greatest in rewarding."

27

It is related that one day the Perwāna, Mu'īnu-'d-Dīn, held a great assembly in his palace. To this meeting were collected together all the Doctors of the Law, the Sheykhs, the men of piety, the recluses, and the strangers who had congregated from various lands.

The chiefs of the law had taken their places in the highest seats. The Perwāna had had a great desire that Jelāl should honour the assembly with his presence. He had a son-in-law, Mejdu-'d-Dīn, governor to the young princes, the sons of the king. This son-in-law of his was a disciple of Jelāl's, and a man of very eminent qualities, with great faith in his teacher. He offered to go and invite Jelāl to the meeting.

Hereupon, the arch-sower of doubts and animosities in the human breast spread among the chiefs of the law, there present, the suspicion that, if Jelāl should come, the question of precedence would arise: "Where should he be seated?" They all agreed that they were themselves in their proper places, and that Jelāl must find a seat where he could.

Mejdu-'d-Dīn delivered the Perwāna's courteous message to his teacher. Jelāl, inviting Husāmu-'d-Dīn and others of his disciples to accompany him, set out for the Perwāna's palace. The disciples went on a little ahead, and Jelāl brought up the procession.

When Husām entered the apartment of the Perwāna, all present rose to receive him, making room for him in the upper seats. Lastly, Jelāl made his appearance.

The Perwāna and other courtiers crowded forward to receive Jelāl with honour, and kissed His Lordship's blessed hands with

170

reverence, expressing regret that he had been put to inconvenience by his condescension. He returned compliment for compliment, and was shown upstairs.

On reaching the assembly room, he saw that the grandees had occupied the whole of the sofa, from end to end. He saluted them, and prayed for God's grace to be showered upon them; seating himself then in the middle of the floor. Husāmu-'d-Dīn immediately rose from his seat, descended from the sofa, and took a place by the side of Jelāl.

The grandees of the assembly now arose also, excepting those who, in spite and pride, had formed the confederacy mentioned above. These kept their seats. Some of them were of the greatest eminence in learning; and one, especially, was not only very learned, but also eloquent, witty, and bold.

He, seeing what had taken place, and that all the men of rank had quitted the sofa, to seat themselves on the floor, asked in a jocose manner: "Where, according to the rules of the Order, is the chief seat in an assembly?"

Some one answered him: "In an assembly of the learned, the chief seat is in the middle of the sofa, where the professor always sits." Another added: "With recluses, the cell of solitude is the chief seat." A third said: "In the convents of dervish brethren, the chief seat is the lower end of the sofa, where, in reality, people put off their shoes."

After these remarks, some one present, as an experiment, asked Jelāl, saying "In your rule and opinion, where is the chief seat?" His answer was: "The chief seat is that where one's beloved is found." The interrogator now asked: "And where is your beloved?" Jelāl replied: "Thou must be blind, not to see."

Jelāl then arose, and began to sing. Many joined; and the singing became so enthusiastic, that the nobles rent their garments.

It so happened that, after Jelāl's death, this interlocutor of his went to Damascus, and there became blind. Friends flocked to visit him, and to condole with him. He wept bitterly, and cried aloud: "Alas, alas! what have I not suffered? That very moment, when Jelāl gave me that fatal answer, a black veil seemed to fall down over my eyes, so that I could not distinguish objects clearly, or their colours. But I have hope and faith in him, that, out of his sublime generosity, he will yet take pity on me, and pardon my presumption. The goodness of the saints is infinite; and Jelāl himself hath said: 'Despair not because of one sin; for the ocean of divine mercy accepteth penitence.'"

The foregoing incident is also related with the following variation:—

Shemsu-'d-Dīn of Tebrīz had just then returned to Qonya, and was among those who accompanied Jelāl to the Perwāna's palace, sitting down near him on the floor. When the question was put: "Where is your beloved?" Jelāl arose, and cast himself on the breast of Shems. That occurrence it was that made Shems, from that time forward, a man of mark in all Qonya.

28

There was in Qonya a great physician, of eminence and ability, who used occasionally to visit Jelāl.

On one of those days, Jelāl requested him to prepare seventeen purgative draughts by a certain time, propitious for taking medicine, as that number of his friends required them.

When the specified time came, Jelāl went to the physician's house, and received the seventeen draughts. He immediately began, and, in the physician's presence, drank off the whole seventeen in succession, thence returning home.

The physician followed him there, to render the assistance he felt sure would be wanted. He found Jelāl seated as usual, in perfect health, and lecturing to his disciples. On inquiring how he felt, Jelāl answered, in the words so often repeated in the Qur'ān: "Beneath which rivers flow." The physician recommended Jelāl to abstain from water. Jelāl instantly ordered ice to be brought and broken up small. Of this he swallowed an inordinate quantity, while the physician looked on.

Jelāl then went to a hot-bath. After bathing, he began to sing and dance; continuing in those exercises three whole days and nights, without intermission.

The physician declared this to be the greatest miracle ever wrought by prophet or by saint. With his whole family, and with many of the greatest in the medical profession, he joined himself to the multitude of Jelāl's disciples of the most sincere.

29

The Perwāna is related to have said publicly, in his own palace, that Jelāl was a matchless monarch, no sovereign having ever appeared in any age like unto him; but that his disciples were a very disreputable set.

These words were reported to them, and the company of disciples were greatly scandalised at the imputation. Jelāl sent a note to the Perwāna, of which the following is the substance:—

"Had my disciples been good men, I had been their disciple. Inasmuch as they were bad, I accepted them as my disciples, that they might reform and become good,—of the company of the righteous. By the soul of my father, they were not accepted as disciples, until God had made Himself responsible that they would attain to mercy and grace, admitted among those accepted of Him. Until that assurance was given, they were not received by me, nor had they any place in the hearts of the servants of God. 'The sons of grace are saved; the children of wrath are sick; for the sake of Thy mercy, we, a people of wrath, have come to Thee.'"

When the Perwāna had read and considered these words, he became still more attached to Jelāl; arose, came to him, asked pardon, and prayed for forgiveness of God, distributing largely of his bounty among the disciples.

30

Another great and good man once observed: "Jelāl is a great saint and a sovereign; but he must be dragged forth from among his disciples." This was reported to Jelāl, who smiled, and said: "If he can!"

Soon afterwards he added: "Why, then, is it that my followers are looked upon with spite by the men of the world? It is because they are beloved of God, and favourably regarded by Him. I have sifted all mankind; and all have fallen through my sieve, excepting these friends of mine. They have remained. My existence is the life of my friends, and the existence of my friends is the life of the men of the world, whether they know this, or whether they ignore it."

31

There was a young merchant, whose house was near Jelāl's college, and who had professed himself a sincere and ardent disciple.

He conceived a desire and intention to make a voyage to Egypt; but his friends tried to dissuade him. His intention was reported to Jelāl, who strictly and rigorously prohibited his undertaking the voyage.

The young man could not divest himself of his desire, and had no peace of mind; so one night he clandestinely stole away, and went off to Syria. Arrived at Antioch, he embarked in a ship, and set sail. As God had willed, his ship was taken by Firengī pirates. He was made prisoner, and was confined in a deep dungeon, where he had a daily portion of food doled out to him, barely sufficient to keep his body and soul together.

He was thus kept imprisoned forty days, during which he wept bitterly, and reproached himself for having been disobedient to the injunction of Jelāl; saying: "This is the reward of my crime. I have disobeyed the command of my sovereign, following after my own evil propensity."

Precisely on the night of the fortieth day, he saw Jelāl in a dream, who addressed him, and said: "To-morrow, to whatever questions these misbelievers may ask thee, do thou return the answer: 'I know.' By that means shalt thou be released." He awoke bewildered, returned thanks to Heaven, and sat down in holy meditation, awaiting the solution of the dream.

Shortly, he saw a company of Firengī people come to him, with whom was an interpreter. They asked him: "Knowest thou aught of philosophy, and canst thou practise therapeutics? Our prince is sick." His answer was: "I know."

They immediately took him out of the pit, led him to a bath, and dressed him in a handsome vestment of honour. They then conducted him to the residence of the sick man.

The young merchant, inspired of God, ordered them to bring him seven fruits. These he prepared with a little scammony, and made the whole into a draught, which he administered to the patient.

By the grace of God, and the intercession of the saints, his treatment was crowned with success, after two or three visits. The Firengī prince recovered; and by reason that the favour of Jelāl was upon that young merchant, though he was utterly illiterate, he became a philosopher. Jelāl assisted him.

When the Firengī prince had entirely recovered his health, and had arisen from his sick-bed, he told the young merchant to ask of him whatsoever he might wish. He asked for his freedom, and for leave to return home, that he might rejoin his teacher. He then related all that had befallen him;—his disobedience, his vision, and the assistance of Jelāl. The whole audience of Firengīs, without sight of Jelāl, became believers in him, and wooers of him.

They set the young merchant free, and allowed him to depart, bestowing on him rich presents and a bountiful outfit.

On his arrival at the metropolis, before going to his own house, he hastened to pay his respects to Jelāl. On beholding the sacred features from afar, he threw himself on the earth, embraced Jelāl's two feet, kissed them, rubbed his face upon them, and wept. Jelāl raised him, kissed both his cheeks, and said: "It was a narrow escape through thy curing the Firengī prince. Thou didst abscond; but henceforward, do thou remain at home, and occupy thyself in earning what is lawful. Take contentment as thy exemplar. The sufferings of the sea, the commotion of the ship, the calamity of captivity, and the darkness of the dungeon, are so many evils. Contentment is a very blessing from God."

32

Jelāl one day was going from his college into the town, when by chance he met a Christian monk, who made him an obeisance. Jelāl asked him which was the elder, himself or his beard. The monk replied: "I am twenty years older than my beard. It came forth that number of years later." Jelāl answered him "Then I pity thee. Thy young beard has attained to maturity, whereas thou hast remained immature, as thou wast. Thou art as black, and as weak, and as untutored as ever. Alas for thee, if thou change not, and ripen not!"

The poor monk at once renounced his rope girdle, threw it away, professed the faith of Islām, and became a believer.

33

A company of black-habited ones (Christian priests or monks) chanced to meet Jelāl one day, as they came from a distant place. When his disciples espied them afar off, they expressed their aversion from them by exclaiming: "O the dark-looking, disagreeable things!"

Jelāl remarked: "In the whole world, none are more generous than they are. They have given over to us, in this life, the faith of Islām, purity, cleanliness, and the various modes of worshipping God; while, in the world to come, they have left to us the everlasting abodes of paradise, the large-eyed damsels, and the pavilions, as well as the sight of God, of which they will enjoy no share; for God hath said 'Verily God hath made both of them forbidden things to the misbelievers!' They walk in darkness and misbelief, willingly incurring the torments of hell. But, let only the sun of righteousness rise upon them suddenly, and they will become believers."

Being now come near enough, they all made their obeisances to Jelāl, entered into conversation with him, and professed themselves true Muslims. Jelāl now turned to his disciples, and added: "God swallows up the darkness in the light, and the light in the darkness. He also makes in the darkness a place for the light." The disciples bowed, and rejoiced.

34

A certain well-known disciple related that, on one occasion, Jelāl and his friends went forth to the country-seat of Husām, and there held a grand festival of holy music and dancing until near daybreak. Jelāl then left off, to give his followers a little rest.

They dispersed about the grounds; and the narrator took a seat in a spot from whence he could see and observe Jelāl. The others all fell asleep; but he occupied himself with reflections on the miracles performed by various of the prophets and of the saints. He thought to himself: "I wonder whether this holy man works miracles. Of course he does; only, he keeps the fact quiet, to avoid the inconveniences of notoriety."

Hardly had the thought crossed his mind, when Jelāl called him by name. On his approaching Jelāl, the latter stooped, picked up a pebble from the earth, placed it on the back of his own hand, and said to him: "Here, take this; it is thy portion; and be thou one of the thankful."

The disciple examined the pebble by the light of the moon, and saw that it was a large ruby, exceedingly clear and brilliant, not to be found in the treasuries of kings.

Utterly astounded, he shrieked out, and swooned away; awaking the whole company with his shout; for he was a very loud-voiced man. On recovery, he told the others what had occurred. He also expressed to Jelāl his contrition for the temerity of his reflections.

Jelāl told him to carry the stone to the queen, and to mention how he had become possessed of it. The queen accepted it, had it valued, and gave to him a hundred and eighty thousand pieces of silver in return, besides rich gifts. She also distributed presents to all the members of the fraternity.

35

A certain sheykh, son of a sheykh, and a man of great reputation for learning, came to Qonya, and was respectfully visited by all the people of eminence residing there.

It so happened that Jelāl and his friends were gone that day to a mosque in the country; and the new-comer, offended at Jelāl's not hasting to visit him, made the remark in public: "Has Jelāl never heard the adage: 'The newly-arrived one is visited'?"

One of Jelāl's disciples chanced to be present, and heard this remark. On the other hand, Jelāl was expounding sublime truths in the mosque to his disciples, when suddenly he exclaimed, "My dear brother! I am the newly-arrived one, not thou. Thou and those like thee are bound to visit me, and so gain honour to yourselves."

All his audience were surprised at this apostrophe; wondering to whom it was addressed. Jelāl then spake a parable: "One man came from Bagdād, and another went forth out of his house and ward; which of the two ought to pay the first visit to the other?"

All agreed in opinion that the man from Bagdād ought to be visited by the other. Then Jelāl explained, thus: "In reality, I am returned from the Bagdād of nulliquity, whereas this dearly beloved son of a sheykh, who has come here, has gone forth from a ward of this world. I am better entitled, therefore, to be visited than is he. I have been hymning in the Bagdād of the world of spirits the heavenly canticle: 'I am the Truth,' since a time anterior to the commencement of the present war, ere the truth obtained its victory." The disciples expressed their concurrence, and rejoiced exceedingly.

By and by, the sheykh's son was informed of this wonder. He at once arose, went on foot to visit Jelāl, uncovered his head, and owned that Jelāl was right. He further declared himself Jelāl's disciple, and said:54 "My father enjoined me to put on ironed sandals, taking an iron-shod staff in my hand, and go forth in quest of Jelālu-'d-Dīn, since it is a duty of all to visit and reverence him who has spoken the truth and reposes on the truth. But the majesty of Jelāl is a hundredfold greater than what my father explained to me."

36

Jelāl once commanded one of his attendants to go and arrange a certain matter. The attendant answered: "God willing."

Upon this, Jelāl was wroth, and shouted to him: "Stupid, garrulous fool!" The attendant fainted and foamed at the mouth.

The disciples interceded. Jelāl expressed his forgiveness; and the attendant recovered.

37

On the occasion of a grand religious commemoration at the house of the Perwāna, in the presence of the Sultan Ruknu-'d-Dīn, this monarch was taken unwell, and the exercises were suspended, only, one of the disciples continued to sing and shout.

The Sultan remarked: "How ill-behaved is that man! Does he pretend to be more ecstatic than his teacher Jelālu-'d-Dīn?"

Jelāl heard this, and answered the king: "Thou art unable to withstand an attack of fever. How then canst thou expect a man devoured with an enthusiasm that threatens to swallow up even heaven itself, to calm down on a sudden?"

When the disciples heard this, they set up a shout; and the Sultan, after himself witnessing one or two of the mighty signs wrought by Jelāl, made his obeisance to him, and became a disciple.

38

It has been related by some that the final overthrow of the rule of the Seljūqī dynasty in Asia Minor (in A.H. 700, A.D. 1300), was in this manner:—

The Sultan Ruknu-'d-Dīn had adopted Jelāl as his (spiritual) father. After a while, he held a great dervish festival in the palace. But, about that period, a certain Sheykh Bāba had created for himself a great name in Qonya, and certain intriguers had led the king to visit him.

It was shortly after that visit that the king held the revival in honour of Bāba in the Hall of the Bowls.

The sheykh was met and introduced in state by the court officials, and was then installed on the throne, with the Sultan seated on a chair by his side. Jelāl now made his appearance, saluted, and took his seat in a corner of the hall. Portions of the Qur'ān were recited, and exhortations were delivered, with hymns.

The Sultan then turned to Jelāl, and spoke: "Be it known to the Lord Jelāl, to the Doctors of the Law, and to the grandees, that I have adopted the Sheykh Bāba as my (spiritual) father, who has accepted me as his dutiful and affectionate son."

All present shouted their approval, and prayed for a blessing on the arrangement. But Jelāl, burning with divine jealousy, instantly exclaimed (in words traditionally related of the prophet, Muhammed): "Verily, Sa'd is a jealous man; but I am more jealous than Sa'd; and God is still more jealous than I am." To this he further added: "Since the Sultan has made the sheykh his father, we will make some other our son." So saying, he gave his usual religious shout of ecstasy, and stalked out from the assembly.

Husāmu-'d-Dīn related that he saw the Sultan, when Jelāl thus quitted the presence, turn pale, as though shot with an arrow.

The grandees ran to stop Jelāl; but he would not return.

A few days afterwards, the officers of state adopted the resolution to invite the Sultan to go to another city, that they might take measures to get rid of Sheykh Bāba. The Sultan now went to consult Jelāl, and ask for his blessing before setting out. Jelāl advised him not to go. The matter had, however, been officially promulgated, and there was no possibility to alter arrangements.

On arriving at the other town, the Sultan was conducted to a private apartment, and forthwith strangled with a bowstring. Ere his breath failed, he invoked the name of Jelāl.

At that moment Jelāl was at his college, lost to consciousness in the enthusiasm of a musical service. Suddenly, he put his two forefingers into his two ears, and ordered the trumpets and chorus to join in. He then shouted vociferously, and recited aloud two of his own odes, of which one commences thus:

My words were: 'Go not; I'm thy friend; the world is rife
With threats of dire destruction; I'm the Fount of Life.'

When the service was over, the disciples requested Jelāl's son,
Sultan Veled, to inquire of his father what all this might signify. In
reply, he merely put off his cloak, and said aloud: "Let us perform
the service for the burial of the dead."

He acted as Precentor in the service, and all present joined in.
Then, without waiting for his son to put any question, he addressed
the assembly, saying: "Yea, Bahā'u-'d-Dīn and my friends! They have
strangled the poor Sultan Ruknu-'d-Dīn. In his agony, he called on
me, and shrieked. God had so ordained. I did not wish his voice to
ring in my ears, and interrupt my devotions. He will fare better in the
other world."

(There is a serious anachronism in the foregoing account.
Sultan Ruknu-'d-Dīn, whose name was Suleyman son of Key-
Khusrew, was put to death by order of the Mogul emperor Abaqa
Khān, in A.H. 664 (A.D. 1265), thirty-six years before the final
extinction of the dynasty by order of Qāzān Khān, between Abaqa
and whom no less than four emperors reigned. Besides this, Jelāl
himself died in A.H. 672 (A.D. 1273), twenty-seven years before
the last of the Seljūqī sovereigns, Key-Qubād son of Ferāmurz son
of Key-Kāwus, was slaughtered, together with all living members
of the race. Historians differ much respecting the names and order
of succession of the last sovereigns of the dynasty; and the present
anecdote shows how confused had become on the spot the legend
of these puppets. Ruknu-'d-Dīn caused his own brother to be
poisoned, as he had become jealous of the favour shown to that
brother by the Mogul emperor. His own death was the reward of
that act.)

39

One day, in lecturing on self-abasement and humility, Jelāl spake a parable from the trees of the field, and said: "Every tree that yields no fruit, as the pine, the cypress, the box, &c., grows tall and straight, lifting up its head on high, and sending all its branches upwards; whereas all the fruit-bearing trees droop their heads, and trail their branches. In like manner, the Apostle of God was the most humble of men. Though he carried within himself all the virtues and excellencies of the ancients and of the moderns, he, like a fruitful tree, was more humble, and more of a dervish, than any other prophet. He is related to have said: 'I am commanded to show consideration to all men, to be kind to them; and yet, no prophet was ever so ill-treated by men as I have been.' We know that he had his head broken, and his teeth knocked out. Still he prayed: 'O our Lord God, guide Thou my people aright; for they know not what they do.' Other prophets have launched denunciations against the people to whom they were sent; and certainly, none have had greater cause to do so, than Muhammed."

"Old Adam's form was moulded first of clay from nature's face;
Who's not, as mire, low-minded's not true son of Adam's race."

In like manner, Jelāl also had the commendable habit to show himself humble and considerate to all, even the lowest; especially so to children, and to old women. He used to bless them; and always bowed to those who bowed to him, even though these were not Muslims.

One day he met an Armenian butcher, who bowed to him seven times. Jelāl bowed to him in return. At another time he chanced upon a number of children who were playing, and who left their game, ran to him, and bowed. Jelāl bowed to them also; so much so, that one little fellow called out from afar: "Wait for me until I come." Jelāl moved not away, until the child had come, bowed, and been bowed to.

At that time, people were speaking and writing against him. Legal opinions were obtained and circulated, to the effect that music, singing, and dancing, are unlawful. Out of his kindly disposition, and love of peace, Jelāl made no reply; and after a while all his detractors were silenced, and their writings clean forgotten, as though they had never been written; whereas, his family and followers will endure to the end of time, and will go on increasing continually.

40

Jelāl once wrote a note to the Perwāna, interceding for a disciple who had been involved in an act of homicide, and had taken refuge in the house of another.

The Perwāna demurred; saying it was a very grave matter, a question of blood. Jelāl thereupon facetiously replied: "A homicide is popularly termed 'a son of 'Azrā'īl (the angel of death).' Being such, what on earth is he to do, unless he kill some one?"

This repartee so pleased the Perwāna, that he pardoned the culprit, and paid himself to the heirs of the slain man the price of his blood.

41

Jelāl one day went forth and preached in the market. Crowds collected round him. But he continued until night fell around him; so he was at length left alone.

The dogs of the market-place now collected in a circle about him, wagging their tails and whining.

Seeing this, Jelāl exclaimed: "By the Lord, the Highest, the Strongest, the All-Compelling One, besides whom none is high, or strong, or powerful! These dogs comprehend my discourse, and the truths I expound. Men call them dogs; but henceforward let them not be so termed. They are of the family of the 'Seven Sleepers.'"

42

The Perwāna much wished Jelāl to give him private instruction at his palace; and requested Jelāl's son, Sultan Veled, to intercede for him in the matter; which he did.

Jelāl replied to his son: "Bahā'u-'d-Dīn! He cannot bear that burden." This was thrice repeated. Jelāl then remarked to his son: "Bahā'u-'d-Dīn! A bucket, the water of which is enough for forty, cannot be drained by one."

Bahā made the reflection: "Had I not pressed the matter, I had never heard this wonderful saying."

43

At another time, the Perwāna, through Bahā'u-'d-Dīn, requested Jelāl to give a public lecture to all the men of science of the city, who were desirous to hear him.

His answer was: "A tree laden with fruit, had its branches bowed down to the earth therewith. At the time, doubts prevented the gardeners from gathering and enjoying the fruit. The tree has now raised its head to the skies, and beyond. Can they hope, then, to pluck and eat of its fruit?"

44

Again, the Perwāna requested Jelāl himself to instruct him and give him counsel.

After a little reflection, Jelāl said "I have heard that thou hast committed the Qur'ān to memory. Is it so?" "I have." "I have heard that thou hast studied, under a great teacher, the Jāmi'u-'l-Usūl, that mighty work on the 'Elements of Jurisprudence.' Is it so?" "It is."

"Then," answered Jelāl, "thou knowest the Word of God, and thou knowest all the words and acts reported of His Apostle. But thou settest them at naught, and actest not up to their precepts. How, then, canst thou expect that words of mine will profit thee?"

The Perwāna was abashed, and burst into tears. He went his way; but from that day he began to execute justice, so as to become a rival of the great Chosroes. He made himself the phœnix of the age, and Jelāl accepted him as a disciple.

45

A company of pilgrims arrived one year at Qonya from Mekka, on their way home elsewhere. They were taken in succession to visit all the chief men of rank and learning in the capital, and were received with every demonstration of respect.

At last they were conducted to Jelāl also, in his college. On seeing him seated there, they all screamed out and fainted away.

When they were recovered, Jelāl began to offer excuses, saying to them: "I fear you have been deceived, either by an impostor, or by some person resembling me in feature. There are men who strongly resemble one another."

The pilgrims one and all objected "Why talks he thus? Why strive to make us doubt our eyes? By the God of heaven and earth, he was with us in person, habited in the very dress he now wears, when we all assumed the pilgrim garb at Mekka. He performed with us all the ceremonies of the pilgrimage, there and at 'Arafāt. He visited with us the tomb of the Prophet at Medīna; though he never once ate or drank with us. Now he pretends that he does not know us or we know him."

On hearing this declaration, Jelāl's disciples were transported with joy, a musical festival ensued, and all those pilgrims became disciples.

46

A certain rich merchant of Qonya, a disciple, as was his wife, of Jelāl's, went to Mekka one year for the pilgrimage.

On the day when the victims are slaughtered, the lady had a dish of sweetmeat prepared, and sent some of it in a china bowl to Jelāl, to be eaten at dinner. She made the request that, when he partook of the food, he would favour her absent husband with his remembrance, his prayers, and his blessing.

Jelāl invited his disciples to the feast; and all ate of the lady's sweetmeat to repletion. But the bowl still remained full.

Jelāl then said: "Oh, he too must partake of it." He took the bowl, ascended to the terraced roof of the college with it, returning immediately empty-handed. His friends asked him what he had done with the bowl and the food. "I have handed them," said Jelāl, "to her husband, whose property they are." The company remained bewildered.

In due course of time, the pilgrims from Qonya returned home from Mekka; and out of the baggage of the merchant, the china bowl was produced, and sent in to the lady, who was much astonished at sight of it. She inquired of her husband how he had become possessed of that identical dish. He replied: "Ah! I also am at a loss to know how it happened. But, on the eve of the slaughter of the victims, I was seated in my tent, at 'Arafāt, with a company of other pilgrims, when an arm projected into the tent, and placed this dish before me, filled with sweetmeat. I sent out servants to see who had brought it to me; but no one was found." The lady at once inferred62 the truth, and guessed what had happened. Her husband was more and more astonished at such miraculous power.

Next day, husband and wife went to Jelāl, stood bare-headed before him, wept for joy, and related what had occurred. He answered:

"The whole thing is the effect of your trust and belief. God has merely made use of my hand as the instrument wherewith to make manifest His power."

47

Jelāl was accustomed to go every year for about six weeks to a place near Qonya, called "The Hot Waters," where there is a lake or marsh inhabited by a large colony of frogs.

A religious musical festival was arranged one day near the lake, and Jelāl delivered a discourse. The frogs were vociferous, and made his words inaudible. He therefore addressed himself to them, with a loud shout, saying: "What is all this noise about? Either do you pronounce a discourse, or allow me to speak." Complete silence immediately ensued; nor was a frog ever once heard to croak again, so long as Jelāl remained there.

Before leaving, he went to the marsh, and gave them his permission to croak again now as much as they pleased. The chorus instantly began. Numbers of people, who were witnesses of this miraculous power over the frogs, became believers in Jelāl, and professed themselves his disciples.

48

A party of butchers had purchased a heifer, and were leading her away to be slaughtered, when she broke loose from them, and ran away, a crowd following and shouting after her, so that she became furious, and none could pass near her.

By chance Jelāl met her, his followers being at some distance behind. On beholding him, the heifer became calm and quiet, came gently towards him, and then stood still, as though communing with him mutely, heart to heart, as is the wont with saints; and as though pleading for her life. Jelāl patted and caressed her.

The butchers now came up. Jelāl begged of them the animal's life, as having placed herself under his protection. They gave their consent, and let her go free.

Jelāl's disciples now joined the party, and he improved the occasion by the following remarks:—"If a brute beast, on being led away to slaughter, break loose and take refuge with me, so that God grants it immunity for my sake, how much more so would the case be, when a human being turns unto God with all his heart and soul, devoutly seeking Him. God will certainly save such a man from the tormenting demons of hell-fire, and lead him to heaven, there to dwell eternally."

Those words caused such joy and gladness among the disciples that a musical festival, with dancing, at once commenced, and was carried on into the night. Alms and clothing were distributed to the poor singers of the chorus.

It is related that the heifer was never seen again in the meadows of Qonya.

49

A meeting was held at the Perwāna's palace, each guest bringing his own waxlight of about four or five pounds' weight. Jelāl came to the assembly with a small wax-taper.

The grandees smiled at the taper. Jelāl, however, told them that their imposing candles depended on his taper for their light. Their looks expressed their incredulity at this. Jelāl, therefore, blew out his taper, and all the candles were at once extinguished; the company being left in darkness.

After a short interval, Jelāl fetched a sigh. His taper took fire therefrom, and the candles all burnt brightly as64 before. Numerous were the conversions resulting from this miraculous display.

50

One day, the poet-laureate, Qāni'ī, came to visit Jelāl at his college. He was the very Khāqānī of the age, and was accompanied by a crowd of noble admirers.

After much conversation, Qāni'ī remarked that he did not like the writings of the poet Sanā'ī, and Jelāl inquired the reason. The poet-laureate replied: "Sanā'ī was not a Muslim." Again Jelāl asked why he had formed that opinion; and Qāni'ī replied: "He has quoted passages from the Qur'ān in his poetry, and has even used them as his rhymes."

Jelāl hereupon rebuked him most severely, as follows:—

65

"Do hold thy peace. What sort of a Muslim art thou? Could a Muslim perceive the grandeur of that poet, his hair would stand on end, and his turban would fall from his head. That Muslim, and thousands such as he,—such as thee,—out of this lower world, and out of the land of spirits, would become real Muslims. His poetry, which is an exposition of the mysteries of the Qur'ān, is so beautifully embellished, that one may apply to it the adage: 'We have drawn from the ocean, and we have poured out again into the ocean.' Thou hast not understood his philosophy; thou hast not studied it; for thou art a Qāni'ī (Follower of one who is satisfied). The vicars of God have a technology, of which the rhetoricians have no knowledge. Hence these truths appear to be imperfect, because men of crude minds are prevented from comprehending them. Though thou hast no part in the lot of the recondite mysteries of the saints, it does not thence follow that thou shouldest deny their position, and so place thyself in a position where destruction may be brought down upon thee. On the contrary, shouldest thou fix thy faith upon them, and act with true sincerity, thou shalt find in the day of judgment no heavy burden on thy shoulders. In lieu thereof, a burden-bearer will be present at thy side,—a refuge, who will prove thy most earnest intercessor."

Struck with these words, the poet-laureate arose, uncovered, begged forgiveness, confessed contrition for his disrespect, and became one of Jelāl's disciples.

A disciple of Husāmu-'d-Dīn wished to make a vow never to do an act not expressly authorised by the Canon Law of Islām. For the purpose of administering the oath to him, instead of the Qur'ān, a copy of the Ilāhī-nāma (Divine Hymns) of the philosopher Sanā'ī was placed on a lectern, covered over with a cloth, and tendered as "the Book" on which he was to swear.

Just then, Jelāl came into the room, and asked what was going on. Husām replied: "One of my disciples is going to make a vow against backsliding. We shrank from swearing him on the Qur'ān, and have therefore prepared a copy of the Ilāhī-nāma for the occasion."

Jelāl observed: "Indeed! Why, the Ilāhī-nāma would draw down on a forswearer a more severe chastisement than the Qur'ān itself. The Word of God is but milk, of which the Ilāhī-nāma is the cream and the butter!"

52

When Adam was created, God commanded Gabriel to take the three most precious pearls of the divine treasury, and offer them in a golden salver to Adam, to choose for himself one of the three.

The three pearls were: wisdom, faith, and modesty.

Adam chose the pearl of wisdom.

Gabriel then proceeded to remove the salver with the remaining two pearls, in order to replace them in the divine treasury. With all his mighty power, he found he could not lift the salver.

The two pearls said to him: "We will not separate from our beloved wisdom. We could not be happy and quiet away from it. From all eternity, we three have been the three compeers of God's glory, the pearls of His power. We cannot be separated."

A voice was now heard to proceed from the divine presence, saying: "Gabriel! leave them, and come away."

From that time, wisdom has taken its seat on the summit of the brain of Adam; faith took up its abode in his heart; modesty established itself in his countenance. Those three pearls have remained as the heirlooms of the chosen children of Adam. For, whoever, of all his descendants, is not embellished and enriched with those three jewels, is lacking of the sentiment and lustre of his divine origin.

So runs the narrative reported by Husām, Jelāl's successor, as having been imparted to him by the latter.

53

A certain flute-player named Hamza, much beloved by Jelāl, happened to die. Jelāl sent some of his disciples to array the defunct in his grave-clothes. He himself followed them to the house of the deceased.

On entering the room, Jelāl addresses the dead body: "My dear friend Hamza, arise!" Instantly, the deceased arose, saying: "Lo, here I am!" He then took his flute, and for three whole days and nights a religious festival was kept up in his house.

Above a hundred Roman misbelievers were thereby converted
to the faith of Islām. When Jelāl left the house, life departed from
the corpse also.

54

Among the disciples there was a hunchback, a devout man, and a
player on the tambourine, whom Jelāl loved.

On the occasion of a festival, this poor man beat his tambourine
and shouted in ecstasy to an unusual degree. Jelāl was also greatly
moved in the spirit with the holy dance.

Approaching the hunchback, he said to him: "Why erectest thou
not thyself like the rest?" The infirmity of the hunch was pleaded.
Jelāl then patted him on the back, and stroked him down. The poor
man immediately arose, erect and graceful as a cypress.

When he went home, his wife refused him admittance, denying
that he was her husband. His companions came, and bare witness to
her of what had happened. Then she was convinced, let him in, and
the couple lived together for many years afterwards.

55

It was once remarked to Jelāl, with respect to the burial service for
the dead, that, from the earliest times, it had been usual for certain
prayers and Qur'ānic recitations to be said at the grave and round
the corpse; but, that people could not understand why he had
introduced into the ceremony the practice of singing hymns during
the procession towards the place of burial, which canonists had
pronounced to be a mischievous innovation.

Jelāl replied: "The ordinary reciters, by their services, bear witness
that the deceased lived a Muslim. My singers, however, testify that he
was a Muslim, a believer and a lover of God."

He added also: "Besides that; when the human spirit, after years of imprisonment in the cage and dungeon of the body, is at length set free, and wings its flight to the source whence it came, is not this an occasion for rejoicings, thanks, and dancings? The soul, in ecstasy, soars to the presence of the Eternal; and stirs up others to make proof of courage and self-sacrifice. If a prisoner be released from a dungeon and be clothed with honour, who would doubt that rejoicings are proper? So, too, the death of a saint is an exactly parallel case."

56

One of Jelāl's chief disciples related that, when he first began to study under that teacher, a company of pilgrims from Mekka came to Qonya, and among them was a very handsome young man of this latter city, son to one of the chief professors there.

This young man brought rich presents to Jelāl, and gifts for the disciples, relating to the latter the following adventure:—

"We were travelling in the desert of Arabia, and I chanced to fall asleep. The caravan went on without me. When I awoke, I found myself alone in the trackless sands. I knew not which way to turn. I wept and lamented for a considerable time, took a direction at hazard, and walked until I was thoroughly exhausted.

"To my surprise and joy I espied a large tent at a distance, with a great smoke rising by it. I made for the tent, and there encountered a most formidable-looking personage, to whom I related my misadventure. He bid me welcome, asked me in, and invited me to rest myself. Within the tent I observed a large kettle, full of fresh-cooked sweetmeat of the finest kind, and a plentiful supply of cool clear water.

"My wonder was great. I asked my host what these preparations might mean, and he answered: 'I am a disciple of the great Jelālu-'d-

Dīn of Qonya, son of Bahā'u-'d-Dīn of Balkh. He is used to pass by here every day. I have therefore pitched this tent for him, and I prepare this food. Perchance, he may honour and bless me with his presence, partaking of hospitality here.'

"As he yet spake, in walked Jelāl. We saluted; and he was begged to partake of the food. He took a little morsel, no larger than a filbert, giving me some also. I fell at his feet, and told him I was from Qonya on pilgrimage, and had missed the caravan by falling asleep. 'Well,' answered he, 'as we are fellow-townsmen, be of good cheer.' He then bade me close my eyes. I did so; and on opening them again I found myself in the midst of my companions of the caravan. I am now come here, on my return home in safety, to offer my thanks for that miraculous kindness, and to profess myself a disciple of the holy man."

57

A man of great learning came once to visit Jelāl. By way of a test, he asked Jelāl two questions: "Is it correct to speak of God as 'a living soul?' since God hath said 'Every living soul shall taste death!'" and: "If one ought not to call God 'a living soul,' what did Jesus mean when he said 'Thou knowest what is in my soul, but I know not what is in Thy soul'?" The second question was: "Can God properly be called 'a thing'? If He can be so called, what is the signification of His word 'Every thing shall perish, save His cause'?"

Jelāl immediately replied: "'But I know not what is in Thy soul' means in Thy knowledge, in Thy absentness, or, as we seers say, in Thy secrecy. Thus the passage would be paraphrased: Thou knowest what is in my secrecy; but I know not what is in the secret of Thy secrecy; or, as 'the people of heart' would put it: Thou knowest what issues from me in the world; but I know not the secret of what issues from Thee in the world to come. It is quite proper to speak of God as 'a thing;' for He hath said 'What thing is greatest in testimony? Say thou: "God;"' i.e., God is the greatest thing in testimony; 'God will be a witness between me and you in the day of the resurrection.' The signification of the passage 'Every thing shall perish' is: every created thing shall perish; not the Creator, i.e., 'save He.' The thing excepted from the general category is 'He.' But God knows best."

The man of learning instantly professed himself a disciple, and composed a panegyric on Jelāl.

58

The legend goes that Jelāl made a practice of seeing the new moon of the Arabian new year, and always uttered the following prayer on seeing it:—"O our Lord God! Thou art the Past-eternal One, the Future-eternal One, the Ancient One! This is a new year. I beg of Thee therein steadfastness to withstand the lapidated Satan,18 and assistance against the rebellious spirit (within me); also, occupation in what will approximate me to Thee, and an avoidance of what might elongate me from Thee. O God! O the All-merciful One, the All-compassionate One! Through Thy mercy, O Most-compassionate of the merciful ones! O thou Lord of majesty and of honour!"

59

It is related that Jelāl cured one of his disciples of an intermittent fever by writing down the following invocation on paper, washing off the ink in water, and giving this to the patient to drink; who was, under God's favour, immediately relieved from the malady:—"O Mother of the sleek one (a nickname of the tertian ague)! If thou hast believed in God, the Most Great, make not the head to ache;

196

vitiate not the swallow; eat not the flesh; drink not the blood; and depart thou out of So-and-So, betaking thyself to some one who attributes to God partners of other false gods. And I bear witness that there is not any god save God, and I testify that Muhammed is His servant and apostle."

60

One day Jelāl paid a visit to a great Sheykh. He was received with the utmost respect, and seated with the Sheykh on the same carpet, both together falling into ecstatic heart-communion with the world of spirits.

A certain dervish was there present also, who had repeatedly performed the pilgrimage at Mekka. The dervish addressed Jelāl, and inquired: "What is poverty?" Jelāl returned no answer; and the question was thrice repeated.

When Jelāl took his leave, the great Sheykh accompanied him to the street door. On his return to his room, he reprimanded the dervish severely for his insolent intrusion on the guest; "especially," said the Sheykh, "as he fully answered thy question the first time thou puttest it." The dervish, surprised, asked what the answer had been. "The poor man," said the Sheykh, "when he hath known God, hath his tongue tied. That is being a real dervish; who, when in the presence of saints, speaks not; neither with the tongue, nor with the heart. This is what is signified by 'Hold ye your peace.' But now, prepare thyself for thy end. Thou art struck by a shaft from heaven."

Three days later, the dervish was met by a gang of reprobates, who attacked and killed him, carrying off every thing he had about him. *Salve fac nos, Domine!*

61

In the days of Jelāl there was in Qonya a lady-saint, named Fakhru-'n-Nisā (the Glory of Women). She was known to all the holy men of the time, who were all aware of her sanctity. Miracles were wrought by her in countless numbers. She constantly attended the meetings at Jelāl's home, and he occasionally paid her a visit at her house.

Her friends suggested to her that she ought to go and perform the pilgrimage at Mekka; but she would not undertake this duty unless she should first consult with Jelāl about it. Accordingly she went to see him. As she entered his presence, before she spoke, he called out to her "Oh, most happy idea! May thy journey be prosperous! God willing, we shall be together." She bowed, but said nothing. The disciples present were puzzled.

That night she remained a guest at Jelāl's house, conversing with him till past midnight. At that hour he went up to the terraced roof of the college to perform the divine service of the vigil. When he had completed that service of worship, he fell into an ecstasy, shouting and exclaiming. Then he lifted the skylight of the room below, where the lady was, and invited her to come up on to the roof also.

When she was come, he told her to look upwards, saying that her wish was come to pass. On looking up, she beheld the Cubical House of Mekka in the air, circumambulating round Jelāl's head above him, and spinning round like a dervish in his waltz, plainly and distinctly, so as to leave no room for doubt or uncertainty. She screamed out with astonishment and fright, swooning away. On coming to herself, she felt the conviction that the journey to Mekka was not one for her to perform; so she totally relinquished the idea.

62

Jelāl was once standing at the edge of the moat round the city of Qonya, when a company of students, undergraduates of one of the colleges in the neighbourhood, seeing him, agreed to try him by asking the question: "Of what colour was the dog of the Seven Sleepers?"

Jelāl's immediate, unpremeditated answer was: "Yellow. A lover is always yellow (sallow); as am I; and that dog was a lover." The students bowed to him, and all became disciples.

63

The Superior of the monks of the monastery of Plato was an old man, and was held in the very highest esteem for his learning in all Constantinople and Firengistān, in Sīs, Jānik, and other lands. (Sīs was capital of the kingdom of Lower Armenia, and Jānik was the secondary "Roman Empire" of Trebizond.) From all those lands did disciples flock to learn wisdom from him.

This Superior related the following anecdote:—

"One day, Jelāl came to the monastery of Plato, situated at the foot of a hill, with a cavern therein, from whence issued a stream of cold water. Jelāl entered the cavern, and proceeded to its farther extremity. The Superior remained at the cavern's mouth, watching for what might happen. For seven whole days and nights Jelāl remained there, seated in the midst of the cold water. At the end of that period he came forth from the cavern, and walked away, singing a hymn. Not the slightest change was apparent in his features, nor in his eyes."

The Superior made oath that all he had read about the person and qualities of the Messiah, as also in the books of Abraham and

Moses, were found in the person of Jelāl, as well as the grandeur and mien of the prophets, as set forth in books of ancient history, and far more besides.

64

Shemsu-'d-Dīn of Tebrīz once asserted, in Jelāl's college, that whosoever wished to see again the prophets, had only to look on Jelāl, who possessed all their qualifications; more especially of those to whom revelations were made, whether by angelic communications, or whether in visions; the chief of such qualities being serenity of mind with perfect inward confidence and consciousness of being one of God's elect. "Now," said he "to possess Jelāl's approbation is heaven; while hell is to incur his displeasure. Jelāl is the key of heaven. Go then, and look upon Jelāl, if thou wish to comprehend the signification of that saying 'the learned are the heirs of the prophets,' together with something beyond that, which I will not here specify. He has more learning in every science than any one else upon earth. He explains better, with greater tact and taste, as also more exhaustively, than all others. Were I, with my mere intellect, to study for a hundred years, I could not acquire a tenth part of what he knows. He has intuitively thought out that knowledge, without being aware of it, in my presence, by his own subtlety."

65

One of the greatest teachers of Qonya was one day giving a lecture on a terraced roof, when suddenly he heard the sound of a lute. He exclaimed: "These lutes are an innovation on the prophetic usages. They must be interdicted."

Forthwith, the form of Jelāl appeared before him, and answered: "That must not be." On this the teacher fainted away.

When he regained his consciousness, he sought to make his peace with Jelāl, by sending an apology and a recantation to him, through the medium of Jelāl's son, Sultan Veled; but Jelāl would not accept them. He answered: "It would be easier to convert seventy Roman bishops to Islām, than to clear away from the mind of that teacher the stains of hate, and so set him on the right road. His soul is as foul as the paper on which children practise their writing exercises."

At length, however, he allowed himself to be appeased by his son; so that he permitted the teacher, with his pupils, to constitute themselves his disciples.

66

Jelāl one day addressed his son, saying "Bahā'u-'d-Dīn, dost thou wish to love thy enemy, and to be loved of him? Speak well of him, and extol his virtues. He will then be thy friend; and for this reason: In like manner as there is a road open between the heart and the tongue, so also is there a way from the tongue to the heart. The love of God may be found by hearing His comely names. God hath said: 'O My servants, take ye heed that ye often commemorate Me, so that sincerity may abound.' The more that sincerity prevails, the more do the rays of the light of truth shine into the heart. The hotter a baker's oven is, the more bread will it bake; if cool, it will not bake at all."

67

Sultan Veled, Bahā'u-'d-Dīn, is said to have recounted of his father, Jelāl, this saying: "A true disciple is he who holds his teacher to be superior to all others. So much so, that, for instance, a disciple of Bāyezīd of Bestām was once asked whether Bāyezīd or Abū-Hanīfa was the greater, and he replied that his teacher, Bāyezīd, was the greater. 'Then,' said the questioner, 'is Bāyezīd the greater, or is Abū-Bekr?' 'My teacher is the greater.' 'Bāyezīd or Muhammed?' 'Bāyezīd.' 'Bāyezīd or God?' 'I only know my teacher; I know no other than him; and I know that he is greater than all others.'

"Another was asked the last question, and his reply was: 'There is no difference between the two.' A third was asked it also, and he replied: 'It would require a greater one than either of the two to determine which of them is the greater.'

"As God does not walk in this world of sensible objects, the prophets are the substitutes of God. No, no! I am wrong! For if thou suppose that those substitutes and their principal are two different things, thou hast judged erroneously, not rightly."

68

Sultan Veled is reported to have said "My grandfather, the Great Master, used to recommend to his disciples to honour his son Jelāl exceedingly, as one of noble extraction and exalted pedigree, of an eternal descent in the past; since the mother of his mother was the daughter of the Imām Sarakhsī, a descendant from Huseyn, son of 'Alī, and grandson of the Prophet."

69

Sultan Veled is also reported to have said: "My father told his disciples that I was seven, and my brother 'Alā'u-'d-Dīn eight years old, when the Dizdār Bedru-'d-Dīn Guhertāsh had us circumcised at Qara-Hisār."

He is also reported to have declared: "When the Sultan invited my grandfather to Qonya, a year passed, and then the Emīr Mūsa invited my grandfather to Larenda, and took my father to be his own son-in-law; so that I was born in that town."

70

Sultan Veled is said to have related that one day, two Turks, law-students, brought to Jelāl an offering of a few lentils, excusing the paucity of the gift, as the result of their poverty. Jelāl thereupon narrated the following anecdote:—

"God revealed to Mustafa (Muhammed) that the believers should contribute of their possessions, for the service of God, as much as they could spare. Some brought the half, some the third part; Abū-Bekr brought the whole of what he possessed. Thus a large treasure was collected, of money, beasts, and arms, for God's service.

"A poor woman, too, brought three dates and a cake of bread—all she had on earth.

"The disciples smiled. Mustafa perceived their action, and said that God had showed him a vision, which he desired to tell to them. They all begged he would favour them with the recital. He therefore thus proceeded:

"'God hath removed the veils from before me. And lo, I saw that the angels had placed in one scale of a balance the whole of your very liberal offerings together, and in the other scale the three dates and one cake of this poor woman. The latter scale was preponderant; its contents outweighed all the rest.'

"The disciples bowed, thanked the prophet, and inquired the hidden explanation of this mystery. He answered: 'This poor woman has parted with her all, whereas my disciples have kept back a part of their possessions. Proverbs say: "The generous one is generous out of what he possesses," and, "A little, in the eyes of the Most Great, is much." You put into the earth a single date-stone, intrusting it to God. He makes that stone become a tree, which yields fruits without number; because the stone was confided to Him. Therefore, let your alms be given to the poor, and to God's servants, as a trust committed unto God. For it is said: "Alms fall first into God's hand, before reaching the hands of the poor;" and again: "Alms for the poor and the destitute.'"

"The poor of Mekka and Medīna, refugees and auxiliaries, shouted their admiration as they heard these words."

When the two Turkish students heard this anecdote related, they professed themselves disciples of Jelāl.

71

When Jelāl was quite young, he was one day preaching on the subject of Moses and Elias. One of his disciples noticed a stranger seated in a corner, paying great attention, and every now and then saying: "Good! Quite true! Quite correct! He might have been the third one with us two!" The disciple surmised that the stranger might be Elias. (Elias is believed by Muslims to be always visible somewhere, but that people know him not. Did they recognise him, they could obtain from him a knowledge of the secret of eternal life, which he possesses.) He therefore seized hold of the stranger's skirt, and asked for his spiritual aid. "Oh," said the stranger, "rather seek assistance from Jelāl, as we all do. Every occult saint of God is the loving and admiring friend of him." So saying, he managed to disengage his skirt from the disciple's hold, and instantly disappeared. The disciple went to pay his respects to Jelāl, who at once addressed him, saying: "Elias, and Moses, and the prophets, are all friends of mine." The disciple understood the allusion, and became more and more devoted at heart to Jelāl than he even was before.

72

It is related that when the burial service was about to be performed over the corpse of Jelāl, the precentor gave a shriek, and swooned away. After a while, he recovered, and then performed his office, weeping bitterly.

On being asked the cause of his emotion, he answered "As I stood forward to perform my office, I perceived a row of the most noble of spiritual saints of the spiritual world, as being present, and as being engaged in reciting the prayers for the dead over the departed one. Those angels of heaven wore robes of blue (the mourning of some sects of Muslims), and wept."

For forty days, that precentor and others daily visited Jelāl's grave.

73

At Damascus, when a young student, Jelāl was frequently seen by others to walk several arrow-flights' distance in the air, tranquilly returning to the terraced roof on which they were standing.

Those fellow-pupils were among his earliest believers and disciples.

74

A friend of Jelāl's once took leave of him at Qonya, and went to Damascus. On his arrival there, he found Jelāl seated in a corner of his room. Asking for an explanation of this surprising phenomenon, Jelāl replied: "The men of God are like fishes in the ocean; they pop up into view on the surface here and there and everywhere, as they please."

75

Jelāl once met a Turk in Qonya, who was selling fox-skins in the market, and crying them: "Dilku! Dilku!" (Fox! Fox! in Turkish.)

Jelāl immediately began to parody his cry, calling out in Persian: "Dil kū! Dil kū!" (Heart, where art thou?) At the same time he broke out into one of his holy waltzes of ecstasy.

76

In the time of Sultan Veled (A.D. 1284-1312), a young man, of the descendants of the Prophet, and son of the guardian of the holy tomb of Muhammed at Medīna, came to Qonya with a company of his fellow-descendants, belonging to that city. He was presented to Sultan Veled, and became his disciple.

He wore a most singular head-dress. One end of his turban hung down in front to below his navel; while the other end was formed into the sheker-āvīz of the Mevlevī dervishes.

When they had become somewhat intimate, Sultan Veled asked him how it happened that he wore the sheker-āvīz of the Mevlevis, when nobody else but those dervishes wear it, in imitation of their founder, Jelāl.

The young man explained that his family were descended from the Prophet. That the Prophet, on the night of his ascension to heaven, after seeing God and many mysteries, had returned a certain distance, and, as is well known, then went back to intercede with God for his people. He now perceived, on the pinnacle of God's throne, the ideal portrait of a form, so beautiful, that he had not hitherto witnessed anything so charming among the angels and inhabitants of heaven.

After contemplating the lovely vision, in amazement, for some time, Muhammed was able to notice that the ideal form wore on its head a sheker-āvīz. He asked Gabriel what that ideal portrait might portend, which was so attractive in its beauty as to surpass all the wonders he had witnessed in all the nine heavens. "Is it the portrait of an angel, a prophet, or a saint?" Gabriel replied "It is the portrait of a personage of the descendants of Abū-Bekr, who will appear in the latter days among the people of thy Church, and will fill the whole world with the effulgence of the knowledge of thy mysteries. To him will God vouchsafe a precedency, and a pen, and a breath, such that kings and princes will profess themselves his disciples; and he will be a most pure upholder of thy religion, being, in every respect, the counterpart of thyself in aspect and in morals. His name will be Muhammed, as is thine; and his surname will be Jelālu-'d-Dīn. His words will explain thy sayings, and will expound thy Qur'ān."

On his return home, the Prophet adopted the form of turban he had seen worn in that ideal portrait, making one end hang down a span in front, and binding the other end behind into a sheker-āvīz.

"From that day to this," said the young man, "the fathers of our family have followed that fashion, so adopted by the Prophet; and we continue to do so too."

It is said that when Abū-Bekr heard this narrative from the Prophet, respecting his great descendant that was thus foretold, he gave the whole of his possessions to the Prophet, to be expended in God's cause.

When Muhammed died, Abū-Bekr wept long and bitterly. But the Prophet appeared to him, and consoled him by saying: "One day I will reappear among my people from out of the collar of one of thy race."

The young man continued: "From that time onwards, our family were on the outlook for the manifestation of the holy personage whose ideal portrait the Prophet so saw. Thank God that I have witnessed the realisation of their hope."

The Qonya pilgrims published this communication to all the disciples there present.

77

In the days of Sultan Veled, a great merchant came to Qonya to visit the tomb of Jelāl. He offered many rich gifts to Sultan Veled, making presents also to the disciples. He related to them many anecdotes of adventures encountered by him in his travels, such as the following:—

He once went to Kīsh and Bahreyn in quest of pearls and rubies. "An inhabitant told me," said he, "that I should find some in the hands of a certain fisherman. I went to him, and the fisher showed me a chest, containing pearls of inestimable value, such as impressed me with astonishment. I asked him how he had collected them; and he told me, calling God to witness, that he, his three brothers, and his father, were formerly poor fishermen. One day they hooked something that gave them immense trouble before they could bring it to land.

"They now found they had captured a 'Lord of the Waters,' also named a 'Marvel of the Sea,' as is commonly known.

"We wondered," said he, "what we could do with the beast. We wept for the ill fortune that had brought us such a disappointment. The creature looked at us as we spoke. Suddenly my father cried out: 'I have it! I will put him on a cart, and exhibit him all over the country at a penny a head!'

"Through the miraculous power of Him who has endowed man with speech and His creatures with life, the beast broke forth and exclaimed: 'Make me not a staring-block in the world, and I will do anything you may wish of me, so as to suffice for you and your children for many years to come!'

"Our father answered: 'How should I set thee free, when thou art so strange and unparalleled a creature?' The beast replied: 'I will make an oath.' Our father said: 'Speak! Let us hear thy oath.'

"The beast now said: 'We are of the faith of Muhammed, and disciples of the holy Mevlānā. By the soul of the Mevlānā, the holy Jelālu-'d-Dīn of Rome, I will go, and I will return.'

"Our father fainted away with astonishment. I, therefore, now asked: 'How hast thou any knowledge of him?' The beast replied: 'We are a nation of twelve thousand individuals. We have believed in him, and he frequently showed himself to us at the bottom of the sea, lecturing and sermonising to us on the divine mysteries of the truth. He brought us to a knowledge of the true faith; so that we continually practise what he taught us.'

"Our father instantly told him he was free. He went back, therefore, into the water, and was lost to sight. But two days later he returned, and brought with him innumerable pearls and precious stones. He asked whether he had been true and faithful to his promise; and on our expressing our satisfaction on that score, he took an affectionate farewell from us.

"We were thus raised from the depths of poverty to the pinnacle of wealth. We became merchant princes, and our slaves are the great merchants of the earth. Every dealer who wishes for pearls and rubies comes to us. We are known as the Sons of the Fisherman. Our father went to Qonya, and paid his respects to the Mevlānā.

"Through his narrative, I formed the design, now carried into effect, to visit the son of that great saint."

This wonderful narrative has been handed down ever since in the mouths of the merchants of Qonya.

78

(The following appears to be an account of one of the first visits of the Perwāna to Jelāl, to whom he subsequently became so devotedly attached.)

One of the most eminent among the men of learning in Qonya was visited by the Perwāna. The learned man held forth eloquently on several exalted themes, and then informed the Perwāna that he had, the night before, been taken up into the highest heaven, and had there learnt many mysteries. He said that he there saw Jelāl hold a higher station of proximity to God than any other saint, as he stood on a level with God's throne.

A day or two later, the Perwāna, filled with reverence for Jelāl's unequalled sanctity, went and paid him a visit with the utmost deference. Before the Perwāna could broach any subject of conversation, Jelāl said to him: "Mu'īnu-'d-Dīn! the vision related to you by your learned friend is quite true in the main facts, though I never saw him there at any time." He then extemporised the following ode:—

Fellow-visitant wert thou? Then say what thou sawest there last night.
Twixt my heart and inspiring loved darling what passed in thy sight?
And if thou, in thy dream, with thy eyes sawest my beautiful love,
Tell us then, in the earrings he wore there what jewels were wove.
If with me thou be fellow in coat, as in thoughts and in creeds,
Let us hear the details of that ragged old mendicant's weeds.
If thou poverty's son be, and unspoken mysteries hear,
Thou'lt recount all the words that were thought by my silent compeer,
If thou'st learnt whence the source of mankind and of souls did proceed.

Since the source was but one, what then means all this search, all this greed?

And if thou hast not seen any place of his form and face free,

Say then what, in the thoughts of his lovers, that face and form be.

And if I head the lists of those lovers, as thou seemest to say,

Tell us, What are those lists? What his messages, words, answers? Pray!

A musical service was then got up, this ode being chanted during its performance. The Perwāna was so utterly bewildered by this incident, that he could say nothing. He therefore rose, bowed, and took his leave.

79

One day, it is said, the Prophet (Muhammed) recited to 'Alī in private the secrets and mysteries of the "Brethren of Sincerity" (who appear to be the "Freemasons" of the Muslim dervish world), enjoining on him not to divulge them to any of the uninitiated, so that they should not be betrayed; also, to yield obedience to the rule of implicit submission.

For forty days, 'Alī kept the secret in his own sole breast, and bore therewith until he was sick at heart. Like a pregnant woman, his abdomen became swollen with the burden, so that he could no longer breathe freely.

He therefore fled to the open wilderness, and there chanced upon a well. He stooped, reached his head as far down into the well as he was able; and then, one by one, he confided those mysteries to the bowels of the earth. From the excess of his excitement, his mouth filled with froth and foam. These he spat out into the water of the well, until he had freed himself of the whole, and he felt relieved.

After a certain number of days, a single reed was observed to be growing in that well. It waxed and shot up, until at length a youth, whose heart was miraculously enlightened on the point, became aware of this growing plant, cut it down, drilled holes in it, and began to play upon it airs, similar to those performed by the dervish lovers of God, as he pastured his sheep in the neighbourhood.

By degrees, the various tribes of Arabs of the desert heard of this flute-playing of the shepherd, and its fame spread abroad. The camels and the sheep of the whole region would gather around him as he piped, ceasing to pasture that they might listen. From all directions, north and south, the nomads flocked to hear his strains, going into ecstasies with delight, weeping for joy and pleasure, breaking forth in transports of gratification.

The rumour at length reached the ears of the Prophet, who gave orders for the piper to be brought before him. When he began to play in the sacred presence, all the holy disciples of God's messenger were moved to tears and transports, bursting forth with shouts and exclamations of pure bliss, and losing all consciousness. The Prophet declared that the notes of the shepherd's flute were the interpretation of the holy mysteries he had confided in private to 'Alī's charge.

Thus it is that, until a man acquire the sincere devotion of the linnet-voiced flute-reed, he cannot hear the mysteries of the Brethren of Sincerity in its dulcet notes, or realise the delights thereof; for "faith is altogether a yearning of the heart, and a gratification of the spiritual sense."

> To *whom, alas, the pangs my love for thee excites, to breathe?*
> *My sighs, like 'Alī, I'll to some deep well's recess bequeathe.*
> *Perchance some reeds may spring therefrom, its brink to overgrow;*
> *Those reeds may moaning flutes become, and so betray my woe.*
> *Who hear will say: 'Be silent, flutes! We're not love's confidants;*
> *To that sweet tyrant make excuse for us and for those plants!'*

80

One of Jelāl's disciples possessed a slave girl of Roman origin, whom Jelāl had named Siddīqa (after Muhammed's virgin wife 'Ā'isha). Occasionally she had miraculous visions. She used to see aureolas of heavenly light, green, red, and black. Various of the angels used to visit her, and souls of the departed.

Her master was vexed at her being so favoured above himself. Once he was visited by Jelāl, and expressed his chagrin to him on the subject. Jelāl replied: "True! There is a heavenly light resides in the pupils of some eyes. These occasionally mislead a few with visions of beauteous form, with which they fall in love. Others they preserve in chastity, and lead them to their adored Maker. Others, again, they may lead to take delight in exterior objects, so as to cast their eyes on every pretty face they see, while the wife at home is curtained away from her husband. Thus, whenever God opens a way to any one, appearing to him, and showing him glimpses of the hidden world, he is apt to become entranced therewith, and to lose all power of further progress, saying to himself: 'How greatly in favour am I!' Others, in short, use every endeavour; but nothing is vouchsafed to them in visions, until they be favoured with a special sight of God Himself, and they be admitted to a near approach unto Him."

The girl's master was comforted, and bowed to his teacher, whose disciples then broke out into a holy service of psalmody and dancing.

81

There was once a wise monk in the monastery of Plato, who was on very friendly terms with Jelāl's grandson 'Ārif. He was very aged, and used to be visited by the dervishes of his neighbourhood, to whom he was very polite, and towards whom he exhibited great confidence; so much so that, one day, some of them inquired of him how he had found Jelāl, and what he had thought of him.

The monk replied to them: "What do you know of him, as to who or what he was? I have seen signs and miracles without number worked by him. I became his devoted servant. I had read in the gospel and in the prophets the lives and the works of the saints of old, and I saw that he compassed them all. I therefore had faith in the truth of his reality.

"One day he came here, conferring on me the honour of a visit. For forty days he shut himself up in ecstatic seclusion. When at length he came forth from his privacy, I laid hold of his skirt, and said to him: 'God, in His holy scripture hath said "And there is none of you but shall come to it (hell-fire)." Now, since it is incontestable that all shall come to the fire of hell, what preference is there in Islām over our faith?'

"For a little time he made no answer. At length, however, he made a sign towards the city, and went away in that direction. I followed after him leisurely. Near the city, we came to a bakehouse, the oven of which was being heated. He now took my black cassock, wrapped it in his own cloak, and threw the bundle into the oven. He then withdrew for a time into a corner, sunk in meditation.

"I saw a great smoke come out of the oven, such that no one had the power of utterance. After that, he said to me: 'Behold!' The baker withdrew the bundle from the oven, and assisted the saint to put on his cloak, which had become exquisitely clean; whereas my cassock was, as it were, branded and scorched, so as to fall in pieces. Then he said: 'Thus shall we enter therein, and thus shall you enter!'

"That selfsame moment I made my bow to him and became his disciple."

82

The reason why the Mesnevī was written is related to have been the following:—

Husāmu-'d-Dīn learnt that several of the followers of Jelāl were fond of studying the Ilāhī-nāma of Sanā'ī, the Hakīm, and the Mantiqu-'t-Tayr of 'Attār, as also the Nasīb-nāma of the latter.

He therefore sought and found an opportunity to propose that Jelāl should indite something in the style of the Ilāhī-nāma, but in the metre of the Mantiqu-'t-Tayr; saying that the circle of friends would then willingly give up all other poetry, and study that alone.

Jelāl immediately produced a portion of the Mesnevī, saying that God had forewarned him of the wishes of the brethren, in consequence of which he had already begun to compose the work. That fragment consisted of the first eighteen couplets of the introductory verses:—

"From reed-flute hear what tale it tells,
What plaint it makes of absence' ills," &c.
It is of the metre Remel, hexameter contracted:

- ‿ - - | - ‿ - - | - ‿ - ‖ - ‿ - - | - ‿ - - | - ‿ - ‖

Jelāl frequently mentions Husām as the cause of the work's having been begun and continued. In the fourth book he addresses him in the opening couplet:—

Of Truth, the light; of Faith, the sword; Husāmu-'d-Dīn aye be;
Above the lunar orb has clomb my Mesnevī, through thee.

And again the sixth book has for its opening verse the following apostrophe:—

"O thou, Husāmu-'d-Dīn, my heart's true life! Zeal, for thy sake,
I feel springs up in me sixth book hereby to undertake."

Often they spent whole nights at the task, Jelāl inditing, and Husām writing down his inspirations, chanting it aloud, as he wrote it, with his beautiful voice. Just as the first book was completed, Husām's wife died, and an interval ensued.

Two years thus passed without progress. Husām married again; and in that year, A.H. 662 (A.D. 1263), the second book was commenced. No other interval occurred until the work was brought to a conclusion. The third couplet of the second book mentions Husām in these terms—

"When thou, of Truth the light, Husámu-'d-Dín, thy courser's rein
Didst turn, descending earthward from the zenith's starry plain."

The third, fifth, and seventh books have similar addresses to Husám
in their opening verses. His name is also mentioned cursorily in the
third tale of the first book.

83

On the death of Jelál, a party of zealots went in a body to the
Perwána, explaining to him that the new practices of music and
dancing, introduced by Jelál, were innovations altogether contrary
to the canonical institutes, and begging him to use his utmost
endeavours to suppress them.

The Perwána called on the learned Mufti of Qonya, Sheykh
Sadru-'d-Dín, and consulted him on the subject. The Mufti's answer
was: "Do nothing of the kind. Listen not to such biased suggestions.
There is an apostolical saying to this effect: 'A laudable innovation,
introduced by a perfect follower of the prophets, is of the same
nature with the customary practices of the prophets themselves.'"
The Perwána resolved, therefore, to do nothing towards suppressing
Jelál's institutions.

84

A certain great man, who esteemed Jelál, was nevertheless shocked
that he should, with all his learning and piety, sanction the use of
music and dancing.

He had occasion to visit Jelál, who at once addressed him as
follows:—"It is an axiom in the sacred canons that a Muslim, if
hard pressed, and in danger of death, may eat of carrion and other
forbidden food, so that the life of a man be not sacrificed. This rule

is admitted and approved by all the authorities of the law. Now, we men of God are exactly in that position of extreme danger to our lives; and from that danger there is no escape, save by song, by music, and by the dance. Otherwise, through the awful majesty of the divine manifestations, the bodies of the saints would melt away as wax, and disappear like snow under the beams of a July sun."

The personage thus addressed was so struck with the earnestness of Jelāl's manner, and the cogency of his reasoning, that he became convinced, and thenceforward was a defender and upholder of Jelāl's institutions, so that these formed, as it were, the very nourishment of his heart. Many of the learned followed his example, and joined themselves to Jelāl's followers and disciples.

85

Kālūmān and 'Aynu-'d-Devla were two Roman painters. They were unrivalled in their art of painting portraits and pictures. Both were disciples of Jelāl.

Kālūmān one day narrated that in Constantinople, on a certain tablet, the portraits of the Lady Meryem and of Jesus were painted, in such style as to be matchless. From all parts of the world artists came and tried their best; but none could produce the equal of those two portraits.

'Aynu-'d-Devla undertook, therefore, to journey to Constantinople, and see this picture. He made himself an inmate of the great church of Constantinople for a whole year, and served the priests thereof in various ways.

One night, then, he spied his opportunity, took the tablet under his arm, and absconded with it.

On reaching Qonya, he paid his respects to Jelāl, who inquired of him where he had been. He narrated to Jelāl all that had occurred with the tablet, which he exhibited.

217

Jelāl found the picture exceedingly beautiful, and gazed on it long with the utmost pleasure. He then spake as follows:—

"These two beautiful portraits complain of you, saying that you are not a faithful admirer of theirs, but are an untrue lover." The artist asked: "How?" Jelāl replied: "They say they are not supplied with food and rest. On the contrary, they are kept sleepless every night, and fasting every day. They complain: 'Aynu-'d-Devla leaves us, sleeps himself all night, and takes his meals by day, never remaining with us to do as we do!'"

The artist remarked: "Food and sleep are to them impossibilities. Neither have they speech, with which to say anything. They are mere lifeless effigies."

Jelāl now replied: "Thou art a living effigy. Thou hast acquired a knowledge of various arts. Thou art the handiwork of a limner whose hand has framed the universe, the human race, and all things on earth and in heaven. Is it right that thou forsake Him, and enamour thyself of an insignificant lifeless effigy? What profit is there in these portraits? What advantage can accrue to thee from them?"

Touched by these reproaches, the artist vowed repentance of his sin, and professed himself a Muslim.

86

When the time of Jelāl's death drew near, he cautioned his disciples to have no fear or anxiety on that account; "for," said he, "as the spirit of Mansūr appeared, a hundred and fifty years after his death, to the Sheykh Ferīdu-'d-Dīn 'Attār, and became the Sheykh's spiritual guide and teacher, so, too, do you always be with me, whatever may happen, and remember me, so that I may show myself to you, in whatever form that may be;—that I may always belong to you, and ever be shedding in your breasts the light of heavenly inspiration. I will simply remind you now that our dear Lord, Muhammed, the

Apostle of God, said to his disciples: 'My life is a blessing unto you, and my death will be a blessing unto you. In my life I have guided you, and after my death I will send blessings on you.'"

Jelāl's friends shed tears all, and broke out into sighs and lamentations; but bowed their heads in reverence.

It is said that he gave directions to get ready his grave-clothes, and that his wife, Kirā Khātūn, began to wail, tearing her clothes, and exclaiming: "O thou light of the world, life of the human race; unto whom wilt thou commit us? Whither wilt thou go?"

He answered her: "Whither will I go? Verily, I shall not quit your circle." She then asked: "Will there be another like unto thee, our Lord? Will another become manifest?" He replied: "If there be, he will be I." After a while he added "While in the body, I have two attachments; one, to you; the other, to the flesh. When, by the grace of the unique Spirit, I become disembodied,—when the world of unbodied spirits, unity, and singleness, shall appear, my attachment to the flesh will become attachment to you, and I shall then have but one sole attachment."

87

With his last breath Jelāl recommended to Husāmu-'d-Dīn to lay him in the upper part of his tomb, so that he might be the first to rise at the last day.

As he lay in his extreme sickness, there were earthquakes for seven days and nights, very severe, so that walls and houses were overthrown. On the seventh occasion, all his disciples were alarmed. He, however, calmly remarked: "Poor earth! it is eager for a fat morsel! It shall have one!"

He then gave his last instructions to his disciples, as follows:— "I recommend unto you the fear of God, in public and in private; abstemiousness in eating and in sleeping, as also in speaking; the avoidance of rebelliousness and of sin; constancy in fasting, continuous worship, and perpetual abstinence from fleshly lusts; long-suffering under the ill-treatment of all mankind; to shun the companionship of the light-minded and of the common herd; to associate with the righteous and with men of worth. For verily 'the best of mankind is he who benefiteth men, and 'the best of speech is that which is short and to the purpose.'"

88

The following is a prayer taught by Jelāl, on his deathbed, to one of his friends, to be used whenever affliction or care might weigh upon him:—

"O our Lord God, I breathe but for Thee, and I stretch forth my spirit towards Thee, that I may recite Thy doxologies abundantly, commemorating Thee frequently. O our Lord God, lay not on me an ailment that may make me forgetful to commemorate Thee, or lessen my yearning towards Thee, or cut off the delight I experience in reciting the litanies of Thy praise. Grant me not a health that may engender or increase in me presumptuous or thankless insolence. For Thy mercy's sake, O Thou Most-Merciful of the compassionate. Amen."

89

A friend was seated by Jelāl's pillow, and Jelāl leaned on that friend's bosom. Suddenly a most handsome youth appeared at the door of the room, to the utmost astonishment of the friend.

Jelāl arose and advanced to receive the stranger. But the friend was quicker, and quietly asked his business. The stranger answered: "I am 'Azrā'īl, the angel of departure and separation. I am come, by the divine command, to inquire what commission the Master may have to intrust to me."

Blessed are the eyes that can perceive such sights!

The friend was near fainting at this answer. But he heard Jelāl call out: "Come in, come in, thou messenger of my King. Do that which thou art bidden; and, God willing, thou shalt find me one of the patient."

He now told his attendants to bring a vessel of water, placed his two feet therein, and occasionally sprinkled a little on his breast and forehead, saying: "My beloved (God) has proffered me a cup of poison (bitterness). From his hand I drink that poison with delight."

The singers and musicians now came in, and executed a hymn, while the whole company of friends wept, and sobbed loudly.

Jelāl observed "It is as my friends say. But, were they even to pull down the house, what use? See my panting heart; look at my delight. The sun sheds a grateful light on the moth. My friends invite me one way; my teacher Shemsu-'d-Dīn beckons me the other way. Comply ye with the summoner of the Lord, and have faith in Him. Departure is inevitable. All being came out of nothing, and again it will be shut up in the prison of nullity. Such is God's decree from all eternity; and, to decree belongeth unto God, the Most High, the All-Great!"

His son Sultan Veled had been unremitting in his attentions. He wept and sobbed. He was reduced to a shadow. Jelāl therefore said to him: "Bahā'u-'d-Dīn, my son, I am better. Go and lie down a little. Rest thyself, and sleep awhile!"

When he was gone, Jelāl indited his last ode; thus:—

Go! head on pillow lay; alone, in peace, me leave,
Loved tyrant, plague by night, while all around thee grieve.
That peerless beauty (God) has no need kind care to show;
But, sallow lovers, ye must patient faith still know.
Perplexity is ours to bear; 'tis his to own hard heart;
Shed he our blood; what sin? He'll not pay murder's smart.

To die's hard, after all; but remedy there's none;
How, then, to crave a remedy? The evil's done.
Last night, in dream, a warder, from my love's abode,
Made sign to me, and said: 'This way! Hold thou my lode.'

90

It is related that, after his death, when laid on his bier, and while he was being washed by the hands of a loving and beloved disciple, while others poured the water for the ablution of Jelál's body, not one drop was allowed to fall to the earth. All was caught by the fond ones around, as had been the case with the Prophet at his death. Every drop was drunk by them as the holiest and purest of waters.

As the washer folded Jelál's arms over his breast, a tremor appeared to pass over the corpse, and the washer fell with his face on the lifeless breast, weeping. He felt his ear pulled by the dead saint's hand, as an admonition. On this, he fainted away, and in his swoon he heard a cry from heaven, which said to him "Ho there! Verily the saints of the Lord have nothing to fear, neither shall they sorrow. Believers die not; they merely depart from one habitation to another abode!"

91

When the corpse was brought forth, all the men, women, and children, who flocked to the funeral procession, smote their breasts, rent their garments, and uttered loud lamentations. These mourners were of all creeds, and of various nations; Jews and Christians, Turks, Romans, and Arabians were among them. Each recited sacred passages, according to their several usages, from the Law, the Psalms, or the Gospel.

The Muslims strove to drive away these strangers, with blows of fist, or staff, or sword. They would not be repelled. A great tumult was the result. The Sultan, the Heir-Apparent, and the Perwāna all flew to appease the strife, together with the chief Rabbis, the Bishops, Abbots, &c.

It was asked of these latter why they mixed themselves up with the funeral of an eminent Muslim sage and saint. They replied that they had learnt from him more of the mysteries shrouded in their scriptures, than they had ever known before; and had found in him all the signs and qualities of a prophet and saint, as set forth in those writings. They further declared: "If you Muslims hold him to have been the Muhammed of his age, we esteem him as the Moses, the David, the Jesus of our time; and we are his disciples, his adherents."

The Muslim leaders could make no answer. And so, in all honour, with every possible demonstration of love and respect, was he borne along, and at length laid in his grave.

He had died as the sun went down, on Sunday, the fifth of the month Jumāda-l-ākhir, A.H. 672 (16th December A.D. 1273); being thus sixty-eight (lunar) years (sixty-six solar years) of age.

92

Sultan Veled is reported to have related that, shortly after the death of his father, Jelāl, he was sitting with his step-mother, Jelāl's widow, Kirā Khātūn, and Husāmu-'d-Dīn, when his step-mother saw the spirit of the departed saint, winged as a seraph, poised over his, Sultan Veled's, head, to watch over him.

93

Jelāl had a female disciple, a saint, named Nizāma Khātūn, an intimate friend of his wife's.

Nizāma formed the design to give a spiritual party to Jelāl, with an entertainment for his disciples. She possessed nothing but a Thevr (or Sevr) veil, which she had destined to be her own winding-sheet.

She now ordered her servants to sell this veil, and so procure the necessaries for the projected feast. But, that same morning, Jelāl came to her house with his disciples, and, addressing her, said: "Nizāma Khātūn, sell not thy veil; to thee it is a piece of necessary furniture. Lo! we are come to thy entertainment."

He and his disciples remained with her, engaged in spiritual exercises, three whole days and nights.

94

After Jelāl's death, Kīgātū Khān, a Mogul general, came up against Qonya, intending to sack the city and massacre the inhabitants. (He was emperor from A.H. 690 to 696, A.D. 1290-1294.)

That night, in a dream, he saw Jelāl, who seized him by the throat, and nearly choked him, saying to him: "Qonya is mine. What seekest thou from its people?"

On awaking from his dream, he fell on his knees and prayed for mercy, seeking also for information as to what that portent might signify. He sent in an ambassador to beg permission for him to enter the city as a friendly guest.

When he arrived at the palace, the nobles of Qonya flocked to his court with rich offerings. All being seated in solemn conclave, Kīgātū was suddenly seized with a violent tremor, and asked one of the princes of the city, who was seated on a sofa by himself: "Who may the personage be that is sitting at your side on your sofa?" The prince looked about, right and left; but saw no one. He replied accordingly. Kīgātū answered: "What? How sayest thou? I see by thy side, seated, a tall man with a grisly beard and a sallow complexion, a grey turban, and an Indian plaid over his chest, who looks at me most pryingly."

The prince sagaciously suspected forthwith that Jelāl's shade was there present by his side, and made answer: "The sacred eyes of majesty alone are privileged to witness that vision. It is the son of Bahā'u-'d-Dīn of Balkh, our Lord Jelālu-'d-Dīn, who is entombed in this land."

The Khān replied: "Last night I saw him in my dream. He went nigh choking me, and told me Qonya is his possession. Now, prince, thee I call my adoptive father; and I entirely forego my intention to devastate this city. Tell me; has that holy man any son or descendant alive here?"

The prince told him of Bahā Veled, now Sheykh of the city, and the peerless saint of God. Kīgātū expressed the wish to go and visit the Sheykh. The prince conducted him and his suite of nobles to Sultan Veled. They all declared themselves his disciples, and assumed the dervish turban. Bahā recounted to the Khān the history of his grandfather's expulsion from Balkh, and of all that followed. The Khān offered him royal presents, and accompanied him on a visit of reverence to the shrine of the deceased saint.

CHAPTER IV

*Shemsu-'d-Dīn Tebrīzī, Muhammed son of 'Alī son
of Melik-dād.*

1

Shemsu-'d-Dīn of Tebrīz was surnamed the Sultan of
Mendicants, the Mystery of God upon earth, the Perfect in
word and deed. Some had styled him the Flier, because he
travelled about so much; and others spoke of him as the Perfect
One of Tebrīz.

He went about seeking for instruction, human and
spiritual. He had visited many of the chief spiritual teachers
of the world; but he had found none equal to himself. The
teachers of all lands became, therefore, pupils and disciples
to him.

He was always in quest of the beloved object of the
soul (God). His corporeal frame he habited in coarsest felt,
shrouding his eminent greatness from all eyes in what are really
the jewelled robes of spirituality.

At Damascus it was, where he was then studying, that he first saw Jelālu-'d-Dīn by chance in a crowded market-place; but Jelāl, who was at that time a student also, avoided him.

Ultimately, he was led to Qonya in Jelāl's traces, and first arrived there at dawn, on Saturday, the twenty-sixth of Jumāda-'l-ākhir, A.H. 642 (28th November, A.D. 1244), Jelāl being then professor at four colleges there. They met as is related in a former chapter

At the end of three months' seclusion together, passed in religious, scientific, and spiritual disquisitions and investigations, Shemsu-'d-Dīn became satisfied that he had never met Jelāl's equal.

2

When Shemsu-'d-Dīn was quite worn out by a series of divine manifestations and the consequent ecstasies, he used to break away, hide himself, and work as a day-labourer at the water-wheels of the Damascus gardens, until his equanimity would be restored. Then he would return to his studies and meditations.

In his supplications to God, he was constantly inquiring whether there was not in either world, corporeal and spiritual, one other saint who could bear him company. In answer thereto, there came at length from the unseen world the answer, that the one holy man of the whole universe who could bear him company was the Lord Jelālu-'d-Dīn of Rome.

On receiving this answer, he set out at once from Damascus, and went in quest of his object to the land of Rome (Asia Minor).

3

Chelebī Emīr 'Ārif related that his father, Sultan Veled, told him that one day, as a trial and test, Shemsu-'d-Dīn requested Jelāl to make him a present of a slave. Jelāl instantly went and fetched his own wife, Kirā Khātūn, who was as extremely beautiful as virtuous and saintlike, offering her to him.

To this act of renunciation Shemsu-'d-Dīn replied: "She is my most esteemed sister. What I want is a youth to wait on me." Jelāl thereupon produced his own son, Sultan Veled, who, he said, would be proud to carry the shoes of Shems, placing them before him for use when required for a walk abroad. Again Shems objected "He is as my son. But, perhaps, you will supply me with some wine. I am accustomed to drink it, and am not comfortable without it."

Jelāl now took a pitcher, went himself to the Jews' ward of the city, and returned with it full of wine, which he set before Shems.

"I now saw," continued Sultan Veled in his recital, "that Shemsu-'d-Dīn, uttering an intense cry, rent his garment, bowed down to Jelāl's feet, lost in wondering admiration at this implicit compliance with the behests of a teacher, and then said: 'By the truth of the First, who had no beginning, the Last, who will have no end, there never has been, from the commencement of creation, and there never, until the end of time, will be, in the universe of substance, a lord and master, heart-captivating and Muhammed-like, as thou art.'"

He now bowed down again, declared himself a disciple to Jelāl, and added: "I have tested and tried to the utmost the patient long-suffering of our Lord; and I have found his greatness of heart to be totally unlimited by any bounds."

4

Jelāl is reported to have said: "When Shemsu-'d-Dīn first came, and I felt a mighty spark of love for him lighted up in my heart, he took upon himself to command me in the most despotic and peremptory manner.

"'Study,' said he, 'the writings of thy father.' For a while I studied nothing else. 'Keep silent, and speak to no one.' I ceased from all intercourse with my fellows.

"My words were, however, the food of my disciples; my thoughts were the nectar of my pupils. They hungered and thirsted. Thence, ill feelings were engendered amongst them, and a blight fell upon my teacher.

"He came to me another day as I was, by his command, studying the writings of my father. Thrice he called out to me: 'Study them not.' From his sacred features the effulgence of spiritual wisdom streamed. I laid down the book, and never since have I opened it."

5

Jelāl is said to have related that Shemsu-'d-Dīn forbade him to study any more the writings of his father, Bahā Veled, and that he punctually obeyed the injunction.

But one night he dreamt that he was in company with a number of friends, who were all studying and discussing with him those very writings of Bahā Veled.

As he woke from his dream, Shems was entering the room with a severe look. Addressing Jelāl, he asked: "How hast thou dared to study that book again?" Jelāl protested that, since his prohibition, he had never once opened his father's works.

"Yes," retorted Shems, "there is a study by reading, and there is also a study by contemplating. Dreams are but the shadows of our waking thoughts. Hadst thou not occupied thy thoughts with those writings, thou wouldst not have dreamt about them."

"From that time forward," remarked Jelāl, "I never again busied myself with my father's writings, so long as Shemsu-'d-Dīn remained alive."

Jelāl is related to have informed his disciples that Shemsu-'d-Dīn was a scholar in every science known to man, and also a great alchemist; but that he had renounced them all, to devote himself to the study and contemplation of the mysteries of divine love.

Shemsu-'d-Dīn was one day sitting with his disciples, when the public executioner passed by. Shems remarked to those around him: "There goes one of God's saints."

The disciples knew the man, and told Shems that he was the common headsman. Shems replied "True! In the exercise of his calling, he put to death a man of God, whose soul he thus released from the bondage of the body. As a recompense for this kind act of his, the saint bequeathed to him his own saintship."

On the following day the executioner relinquished his office, vowed repentance, came to Shemsu-'d-Dīn, made his bow, and professed himself a disciple.

8

Sheykh Husāmu-'d-Dīn was originally a young man who showed great respect and humility towards Shemsu-'d-Dīn, to whom he rendered services of every kind.

One day Shems said to him: "Husām, this is not the way. Religion is a question of money. Give me some coin, and offer your services to the Lord; so, peradventure, thou mayest rise in our order."

Husām at once went forth to his own house, collected all his own valuables and money, with his wife's jewels, and all the provisions of the house, brought them to Shems, and laid them at his feet. He furthermore sold a vineyard and country-seat he possessed, bringing their price also to his teacher, and thanking him for having taught him a duty, as also for having deigned to accept so insignificant a trifle from his hand.

"Yes, Husām," said Shems "it is to be hoped that, with God's grace, and the prayers of the saints, thou wilt henceforth attain to such a station, as to be the envy of the most perfect men of God, and be bowed down to by the Brethren of Sincerity. It is true that God's saints are not in want of anything, being independent of both worlds. But, at the outset, there is no other way to test the sincerity of one we love, and the affection of a friend, than to call upon him to sacrifice his worldly possessions. The next step is, to summon him to give up all that is not his God. No disciple who wishes to rise, has ever made progress by following his own devices. Advancement is earned by rendering service, and by spending in God's cause. Every pupil who sacrifices possessions at the call of his teacher, would also lay down his life, if needs were. No lover of God can retain both mammon and religion."

Shems then restored to Husām the whole of his goods, keeping back only one piece of silver. Nine times as much more did he bestow upon Husām from first to last; and, as the results of all things are in God's hands, so did Husām at length become the ruler of God's saints, and Jelāl made him the keeper of God's treasury. He it was who wrote down the twenty-four thousand six hundred and sixty couplets contained in the six books of the Mesnevī.

9

Shemsu-'d-Dīn left Qonya, at the end of his first visit, on Thursday, the twenty-first day of the month of Shawwal, A.H. 643 (14th March, A.D. 1246), after a stay of about sixteen months.

He returned to Damascus; and his departure left Jelāl in a state of great uneasiness and excitement. (Compare a conflicting date given in No. 13, further on.)

10

Shemsu-'d-Dīn was one day at Bagdād, and entered one of the palaces there. A eunuch who saw him enter, without being himself visible, made a sign to a slave to go and drive away the mendicant.

The slave drew his sword, and raised it to strike; but his arm withered, and fell palsied.

The eunuch then motioned to another slave to execute the commission; and he, too, became similarly incapacitated.

Shems then went away of himself, and none dared to pursue him. Two days later, the eunuch died also.

11

Jelāl's father, Bahā Veled, had a disciple, who, for some reason, gave offence to Shemsu-'d-Dīn; the latter, in punishment, inflicted a deafness on both the disciple's ears.

After a time, Shems pardoned the offender, and restored his hearing. But the man bore him a grudge in his heart, nevertheless. One day, Shems said to him: "Friend, I have pardoned thee; wherefore art thou still cast down? Be comforted." Notwithstanding this, his rancour remained.

One day, however, he met Shems in the midst of a market. Suddenly, he felt a new faith glow within him, and he shouted out: "There is no god save God; Shemsu-'d-Dīn is the apostle of God."

The market-people, on this, raised a great hubbub, and wished to kill him. One of them came forward to cut him down; but Shems uttered so terrific a shout, that the man at once fell down dead. The rest of the market-people bowed, and submitted.

Shems now took the disciple by the hand, and led him away, remarking to him: "My good friend, my name is Muhammed. Thou shouldest have shouted: 'Muhammed is the apostle of God.' The rabble will not take gold that is not coined."

12

One beautiful moonlight night, Jelāl and Shems were together on the terraced roof of the college, and all the inhabitants of Qonya were sleeping on their housetops.

Shems remarked: "See all these poor creatures! They are dead to every sense of their Creator on this beautiful night of God's decree. Wilt thou not, Jelāl, of thy infinite compassion, wake them up, and let them gain a share in the shower of blessings of this night?"

Thus appealed to, Jelāl faced toward Mekka, and offered up this prayer to God: "O Thou Lord of heaven, and of earth, for the love of Thy servant Shemsu-'d-Dīn, vouchsafe wakefulness to this people."

Immediately a black cloud gathered from the unseen world. Thunders and lightnings burst forth; and so heavy a rain fell, that all the sleepers, catching up what clothing they could find, quickly took refuge in their106 houses below. Shems smiled at the saintly joke, and was greatly amused.

When daylight dawned, the disciples gathered round, numerous as the raindrops of that shower; and Shems related to them the story, with the following remarks:—

"Hitherto, all the prophets and saints have ever sought to hide from vulgar eyes the miraculous powers they have possessed, so that none should be aware of the fact. But now, our Lord and Master, Jelāl, has been so successful in secretly following up the path of mystic love, that his miraculous powers have hitherto escaped the searching eyes of even the chiefest of God's elect, even as it hath been said: 'Verily, God hath saints of whom no man knoweth.'"

13

Kimiyā Khātūn, the wife of Shemsu-'d-Dīn, was a very beautiful, and also a very virtuous, woman. One day, however, it so happened that, without his permission or knowledge, the grandmother of Sultan Veled, and her attendant ladies, took Kimiyā with them for an outing to the vineyards of the city.

As chance would have it, Shems came home while she was still away. He asked for her, and was informed where she had gone, and with whom. He was exceedingly annoyed at her absence.

Kimiyā had scarcely returned home, ere she began to feel unwell. Her limbs stiffened like dry firewood, and became motionless. She continued screaming and moaning for three days, and then gave up the ghost, in the month of Sha'bān, A.H. 644.

14

It is related that, a second time, Shems and Jelāl shut themselves up for a whole six months in Jelāl's room at the college, without partaking of meat or drink, and without the entrance of a single individual to interrupt them, or either of them coming forth, Sultan Veled and one other disciple alone excepted.

15

Shemsu-'d-Dīn was extremely bitter in his preachings and lectures to the learned auditory who used to gather around him in Qonya. He likened them to oxen and asses. He reproached them with being

further than ever astray from the path of living love, and taxed them
with the presumption of supposing themselves the equals of Bāyezīd
of Bestām.

He once went to Erzen-of-Rome (Erzrūm), the prince of which
city had a son so extremely stupid, though very handsome, that he
could be taught nothing, or next thereto.

Shems let no one know who or what he was; but opened a
school for children. Inquiries were made by the prince, and Shems
undertook to instruct the child, and enable him, in one month, to
recite the whole Qur'ān by heart.

He kept his promise. The young prince acquired, further,
during the same period, a beautiful handwriting, and sundry other
accomplishments.

It began to be suspected, now, that he was a saint in disguise. He
therefore quietly slipped away from that city.

16

There is a tradition that Jelāl one day called his son Sultan Veled,
gave him a large sum of money, and bade him go, with a suite of the
disciples, to Damascus, and request Shems to return to Qonya.

Jelāl told his son that he would find Shems in a certain inn,
playing at backgammon with a young Firengī (European, Frank),
also one of God's saints. Sultan Veled went, found Shems exactly
so occupied, and brought him back to Qonya, the Firengī youth
returning to his own country, there to preach Jelāl's doctrines, as
his vicar.

Sultan Veled walked the whole way from Damascus to Qonya, at
the stirrup-side of Shems, as a groom walks by the side of a prince's
charger. The whole city went forth to receive them. Jelāl and Shems
embraced each other. Jelāl became more than ever devoted to his
friend; and his disciples resented his neglect of them, as they had

done before. Not long afterwards, the dolorous event occurred that terminated the life of Shemsu-'d-Dīn.

17

The Vazīr of Qonya had built a college. On its completion, he gave a great entertainment, in the college, of religious music and dancing, all the learned men of the city being present.

The Qur'ān was first recited in its entirety; after which, the holy waltzing began. The Vazīr and Shemsu-'d-Dīn both joined in the dance. Several times they came into collision; or, the Vazīr's skirt swept against Shems's person, as he observed no caution in his gyrations.

Jelāl expressed great indignation at this want of courtesy and reverence for his guest and friend. He took Shems by the hand, to lead him away. The grandees present essayed to appease him, but their entreaties were of no avail. The police of the Sultan were therefore sent for; and when they arrived, they instantly seized Shems, led him forth a prisoner with every mark of indignity, and put him to death without further inquiry or formality.

18

Chelebī Emīr ʿĀrif related, as informed by his mother, Fātima Khātūn, that when Shemsu-'d-Dīn was thus made a martyr, his executioners threw his corpse down a well.

Sultan Veled saw Shems in a dream, and was informed by him where the body would be found. Sultan Veled went therefore at midnight with some friends, recovered the corpse, washed it, and privately buried it in the college grounds, by the side of the founder.

19

Forty days after the disappearance of Shemsu-'d-Dīn, Jelāl, wishing to appease his own sorrow, and quell the mutinous spirit that had broken out among the disciples, appointed Husāmu-'d-Dīn his local deputy, and set out to seek Shems at Damascus for the third time. All the learned men of Syria became his disciples, and he was absent about a year, more or less.

The Sultan and the nobles grew impatient at this long absence, and wrote him an urgent petition, begging him to return to Qonya. With this request he complied.

Naturally, he had failed to find Shemsu-'d-Dīn in the flesh at Damascus; but he had found within himself what was still greater. He went to the lodging of Shems, and wrote on the door, with red ink: "This is the station of the beloved one of Elias, on whom be peace!"

It is said that the body of Shemsu-'d-Dīn disappeared, and that he was buried by the side of Jelāl's father, Sultan Bahā Veled the Elder.

CHAPTER V

Sheykh Salāhu-'d-Dīn26 Ferīdūn, surnamed
Zer-Kūb (Goldbeater).

1

Sheykh Salāhu-'d-Dīn was originally a fellow-disciple with Jelāl, as pupils to Seyyid Burhānu-'d-Dīn. He afterwards became a goldbeater, as his parents were poor.

After a while, when Jelāl's reputation became great, Salāh went and paid him his respects. Jelāl knew how highly Burhān had esteemed Salāh, when his pupil. He therefore received him in a very friendly manner, and their intercourse became warmly renewed.

One day, after the murder of Shemsu-'d-Dīn, and the return of Jelāl from Damascus, he sent for Salāh, and appointed him his own assistant in the government and instruction of the disciples, presenting him also to the king in that capacity.

2

Jelāl's first royal protector, 'Alā'u-'d-Dīn Keyqubād, was now dead, and his son, Gayāsu-'d-Dīn Key-Khusrev, reigned in his stead.

The monarch one day made a feast in the vineyards, and went forth into the fields for a walk, alone. He picked up a young snake, carried it indoors, placed it in a gold box, sealed this up, and then rejoined his courtiers.

To those attendants the king exhibited the sealed packet, as having just then been privately received from the Qaysar of Constantinople with a message to this effect: "If your religion of Islām be the true faith, some one of your wise men will be able to see into this packet without breaking its seals, and to tell what it contains."

The king then called upon his ministers to prove their loyalty to him, and their faithfulness to their religion, by solving this riddle. None of them was able.

The packet was now sent round in succession to all the eminent teachers and theologians of the city; but none could unravel the enigma.

At last it was brought to Jelāl, as Sheykh Ferīdūn and he were sitting together. Jelāl invited Ferīdūn to tell them the contents of the packet; and he immediately replied: "It is not a dignified act in the king to imprison a young snake in a gold box, sealing this up as a packet, and then tempting his courtiers, ministers, and learned men with a false pretence. A saint, however, knows not only the solution of so paltry a trick as this, but is also aware of every thought in the king's heart, and every secret of earth and heaven."

When this answer was reported to the king, he came to the college, and professed himself a disciple, remarking: "If the disciples of Shemsu-'d-Dīn possess such power, and work such miracles, how great must have been the sanctity of the murdered martyr."

Ferīdūn acted for ten years as assistant to Jelāl.

Fātima, the daughter of Sheykh Salāhu-'d-Dīn Ferīdūn, was married to Sultan Veled, Jelāl's son. Jelāl used to teach her to read the Qur'ān and other books.

Jelāl used to call Fātima his right eye; her sister Hediyya, his left eye; and their mother, Latīfa Khātūn, the personification of God's grace.

When Fātima's marriage was solemnised, all the angels of heaven were present, and wished the young couple all happiness.

She was a saint, and continually worked miracles. She fasted by day and watched by night, tasting food only once in three days. She was very charitable to the poor, the orphans, and the widows, distributing to them food and raiment.

Sheykh Ferīdūn died on New Year's Day, A.H. 657 (28th December, A.D. 1258).